THE COLORS OF SUBMISSION

Learning to Submit to God

Wayne P. Cooper

D1715060

ISBN-13: 978-1-9832-2649-6

About *The Colors of Submission*

"*The Colors of Submission* is not a weighty tome filled with the theoretical aspects of submission to God. It is rather a well-written, brisk-paced, biblically-saturated travel guide for those actually trekking the path of submission, by someone who is walking it with them. In writing this volume and breaking down submission to God into its nitty-gritty components, Wayne Cooper has done a great service to the church and to her Lord. I speak personally: I faced a situation in which I needed it the day after I read it. Read it for yourself and allow it to help you journey into deeper submission."

> —**Timothy Berrey**, Missionary in the Philippines with Gospel Fellowship Association

"In *The Colors of Submission: Learning to Submit to God,* Pastor Wayne Cooper speaks to our hearts about why we do what we do. He helps us understand how we can please the Lord in a greater way with the decisions we make in life. Many of our daily struggles are addressed with solid biblical answers and guidance. Having known Wayne and Charity for many years, I can say that they both are living out their faith having learned to submit to the Lord through some of the hardships in life. Whether you are a new Christian or seasoned in the ministry by years of hardships, you will find encouragement, instruction, and help in this book."

> —**Scott Wendal**, Senior Pastor, Valley Forge Baptist Temple, Collegeville, Pa.

"Christians know that they need to submit to God, but often they do not know how. Wayne Cooper has answered how by breaking down the act of submitting to God into its component parts as an aid to help believers fully submit to God. *The Colors of Submission* helps anyone who wants to more deeply understand how to walk in submission to God. It is an excellent resource for pastors and biblical counselors to add to their toolbox."

> —**Don Harrelson**, Pastor, Cumberland Bible Church, Cumberland, Md.

DEDICATION

To my wife, Charity, whose loving submission to her Lord and to her husband has helped make our marriage beautiful.

CONTENTS

ACKNOWLEDGEMENTS

I now know firsthand that no book can be completed without help, and I am extremely grateful to those who have assisted me with this book in one way or another.

First, I thank the members of my church who heard this content in a series of messages and offered their feedback both visually and verbally.

Second, I am grateful for my wife who continually encouraged me in this project and provided her meticulous proofreading skills.

Third, I thank Don Harrelson, my good friend, whose editorial skills proved invaluable to me.

Finally, I offer my broad thanks to my many friends—too many to name—who knowingly and unknowingly encouraged me as I wrote. The Lord used your kind words to keep me at the task.

Of course, my greatest thanks and praise belong to my Lord and Savior, who placed this study on my heart and taught me these lessons from his Word so that I could teach others. Without his work in me, this book would not exist.

PREFACE

I had always considered myself a submissive person. Growing up, I was a fairly obedient child, giving my parents little trouble. I never fought against God's will for my life. When he called me into the ministry, I answered the call gladly. But the Lord has his ways of bringing us face to face with our deficiencies, and he showed me how much I truly lacked submission.

That revelation came to me through the life of a young man in my church whom I was discipling. The more that I worked with Jacob, the more that I marveled at his submissive attitude—towards me, towards his parents, and towards God. At the same time, the Lord brought a series of personal challenges into my life, and I began to wrestle with God's will.

I remember one day in which I had asked Jacob to share with me his prayer requests, and after doing so, he turned the question on me. I replied, "Oh, Jacob, I have many needs." Whether my answer was merely an evasion of his question or a test of his sincerity in asking, I cannot say. But he did not allow me to evade. He replied, "Fill in the blank: you can pray for _____." Immediately, the Holy Spirit brought something to the forefront of my mind. I looked at Jacob and studied him. Could I trust him with so personal a request? I decided that I could. "Jacob," I said, "I admire your submission. That's something I need. You can pray that I'll become more submissive."

He did and has continued in that prayer for me. This book is part of the answer to his prayers; for out of those prayers, this study was awakened in me. As for the lessons in my own life, I'm still trying to learn them, but I'm finding the journey to be sweet. I hope you will join me!

Wayne P. Cooper
Pine Grove, West Virginia

INTRODUCTION

L ight usually appears bright and white, but if it is put through a prism, it is broken into colors. No longer do you see white. Rather, you see the rainbow. Thus, something as beautiful as light is seen in all its facets, making it even more beautiful than before.

Submission is a beautiful quality, but the comprehending of it is sometimes as difficult as the makeup of sunlight. The attaining of it has been given up by many as impossible. Yet, it is clearly commanded in the Scriptures in several relationships, the greatest being our relationship with God. James said, "Submit yourselves therefore to God" (James 4:7a).

But what if you could put submission through a spiritual prism? What "colors" would be reflected from its light? This is what I aim to do in this book. With the Word of God as your prism, you can discover the facets of submission.

The Bible is full of characters who display the colors of submission, and if you desire to achieve a certain grace in your own life, it is wise to study those saints of old who possessed it. But in spite of such beautiful examples of submission, such as Abraham in the Old Testament or Paul in the New Testament, there is only one man who provides the full spectrum of color. That one is Jesus. Only Jesus' submission is perfect. Thus, while the others are worth studying because of the enhancement they bring to the color, Jesus' example is supreme. You and I must seek to be like him.

THE COLORS OF SUBMISSION

Submission is...

ARRANGEMENT, *which requires*

OBEDIENCE. *But since I struggle to obey, I need*

SURRENDER. *And I will only come to that by*

TRUST,

HUMILITY, *and*

REVERENCE. *This must be followed with*

PERSEVERANCE *and*

CONTENTMENT, *after which I shall experience*

JOY.

CHAPTER 1 - ARRANGEMENT

L et me speak with the manager, please." You have probably heard or possibly spoken those words. Often, they are the words of a frustrated customer who is trying to get a problem resolved. Unable to achieve his end with an ordinary worker, the customer decides to go to the top. Nearly every human institution has some sort of authority structure with a chain of command—an arrangement. This is the first element of submission.

The Meaning of the Word

The Greek verb translated "submit" in the New Testament is *hupotassō*, which is a compound word. The root of the word means "to put in order," while the prefix means "under." Together, they denote "to arrange under." In fact, this word was a Greek military term for the arrangement of troops under commanders in their various divisions.[1] The military is an excellent example for the arrangement of submission because the ranks are kept and maintained with strict order. Everyone in the military knows his place and the behavior expected towards his superiors.

The Arrangement of the World

The verb *hupotassō* appears six times in 1 Corinthians 15:27-28 (bolded for emphasis):

> For he **hath put** all things **under** his feet. But when he saith all things are **put under** him, it is manifest that he is excepted, which **did put** all things **under** him. And when all things **shall be subdued** unto him, then shall the Son also himself **be subject** unto him that **put** all things **under** him, that God may be all in all.

The New American Standard Bible captures the repetition better by using the same English word:

> For he has put all things in **subjection** under his feet. But when he says, "All things are put in **subjection**," it is evident that he is excepted who put all things in **subjection** to him. And when all things are **subjected** to him, then the Son himself also will be **subjected** to the one who **subjected** all things to him, that God may be all in all.

Describing the arrangement of the world, these verses tell us that everything has been put under the feet of Jesus—subjected to him. It was for this reason, that Jesus was able to stand up in a boat on the Sea of Galilee in the midst of a violent storm, cry out, "Peace, be still," and the wind and the waves obeyed him (Mark 4:39). They had no choice; they had been subjected to Christ.

Peter tells us that "angels and authorities and powers [have been] made subject unto him" (1 Pet. 3:22). This would include all angelic powers both good and bad. For this reason, Jesus always was able to cast out the demons that possessed and tormented people. The disciples tried and sometimes failed (Matt. 17:16-18), but Jesus never failed. The demons were subject to him and could not even so much as argue when he told them to leave.

Paul declared that God has put all things under Christ's feet "and gave him to be the head over all things to the church" (Eph. 1:22). The church has been made subject to Jesus Christ. Therefore, Jesus declared to his disciples, who were to found the church a few short days after his ascension: "All authority has been given to me in heaven and on earth. Go therefore and make disciples of all nations" (Matt. 28:18-19a NKJV).

Each of these verses demonstrates the arrangement of the world; everything is under Christ. Everything is to be in submission to him.

The Example of Jesus

Yet, 1 Corinthians 15:28 also says that Jesus is subjected to the Father. As you study the Gospels, you realize that Jesus lived his life on this earth in complete submission to God.

Sitting by the well outside the Samaritan city of Sychar, Jesus had been conversing with a Samaritan woman, whose reputation was less than admirable. After she returned excitedly to the city with her new found faith in Christ, Jesus' disciples urged him to eat. He replied, "I have meat to eat that ye know not of." Of course, this confused the disciples who could only think of filling their empty stomachs at the moment. Jesus clarified, "My meat is to do the will of him that sent me, and to finish his work" (John 4:32, 34).

In the next chapter of John, Christ said, "I can of mine own self do nothing: as I hear, I judge: and my judgment is just; because I seek not mine own will, but the will of the Father which hath sent me" (5:30). Then, he emphasized it again, "For I came down from heaven, not to do mine own will, but the will of him that sent me" (6:38). Jesus said that his "meat" (food) was to do God's will. In fact, he sought no other will than God's will and refused to do any other will than the will of the Father, who had sent him.

To do the will of his Father was Jesus' attitude throughout life. When he was a boy of twelve, on the cusp of manhood, he had attended the Passover feast in Jerusalem. Being completely taken up with the holy city, Jesus unwittingly stayed behind to absorb the instruction of the religious teachers. When the worried Joseph and Mary finally found him and scolded him, Jesus replied, "Didn't you know that I had to be about my Father's business?" Even as a child, Jesus knew that God was his Father (in a unique way) and that God had given him a mission to fulfill. But the age of twelve was not the time to embark upon that mission. Therefore, "he went down with them, and came to Nazareth, and was subject unto them" (Luke 2:51a).

Jesus was in complete submission in his earliest years. He was submissive in the midst of his ministry. And he was fully submissive at the end of his life. He had testified at the well of Sychar that his will was to do God's work *and finish it.* Later, as he prayed with his disciples before his arrest, he declared, "I have finished the work which thou gavest me to do" (John 17:4b). Then, as he hung upon the cross, he triumphantly announced, "It is finished" (John 19:30). It was submission to the end!

Yet, all the while that Jesus lived in complete submission to the Father, everything else was subject to him. When Peter tried to defend Jesus in the Garden of Gethsemane with his sword, Jesus rebuked him. "Put up again thy sword into his place: for all they that take the sword shall perish with the sword. Thinkest thou that I cannot now pray to my Father, and he shall presently give me more than twelve legions of angels?" (Matt. 26:52-53). As the old song says, "He could have called ten thousand angels to destroy the world and set him free."[2] They were at his beckon, but he did not call them for one simple reason: "But how then shall the scriptures be fulfilled, that thus it must be?" (Matt. 26:54). In essence, Jesus was saying, "How will I fulfill the will of God and finish the work of God (the redemption of man) if I don't submit to the cross."

Jesus lived in perfect alignment under God. He had arranged Himself in that position in order to fulfill God's purpose, and he never once deviated from it. There was a time when in the far northern regions of Galilee at Caesarea Philippi, Jesus described how he would have to die in Jerusalem. Such a thought was unthinkable to Peter, and he took his Lord aside and rebuked him, "This isn't going to happen to you." Jesus was undaunted; turning to Peter, he said, "Get thee behind me, Satan: thou art an offense unto me: for thou savourest not the things that be of God, but those that be of men" (Matt. 16:23). Anything other than the will of God was an offense to Christ. That is the arrangement of submission.

What About You?

The life of Christ demonstrates that true submission is first an attitude before it is an action. True submission recognizes its God-given place and then gets into that place. This attitude is critical because most of the relationships in which submission is required have an authority structure. The Bible commands submission in at least seven relationships:

1. Believers to God (James 4:7)
2. Wives to husbands (Eph. 5:22)
3. Children to parents (Eph. 6:1, cf. Luke 2:51)
4. Servants to masters (1 Pet. 2:18)
5. Citizens to government (Rom. 13:1)
6. Believers to other believers, particularly church leaders (Eph. 5:21 with Heb. 13:7, 17)
7. Younger people to older people (1 Pet. 5:5)[3]

All of these relationships involve arrangement. You must arrange yourself under the one whom God has placed over you. And at the top of this chain of command is God.

> But I would have you know, that the head of every man is Christ; and the head of the woman is the man; and the head of Christ is God. (1 Cor. 11:3)

> Masters, give unto your servants that which is just and equal; knowing that ye also have a Master in heaven. (Col. 4:1)

> Let every soul be subject unto the higher powers. For there is no power but of God: the powers that be are ordained of God. (Rom. 13:1)

And he [Christ] is the head of the body, the church: who is the beginning, the firstborn from the dead; that in all things he might have the preeminence. For it pleased the Father that in him should all fullness dwell. (Col. 1:18-19)

Your submission in the other relationships of life ultimately is a reflection of your submission to God, who is at the top. Peter declares, "Submit yourselves to every ordinance of man **for the Lord's sake**: whether it be to the king, as supreme; or unto governors, as unto them that are sent by him for the punishment of evildoers, and for the praise of them that do well" (1 Pet. 2:13-14). If you struggle to submit in a human relationship, you are out of line in your relationship with God. That is why submitting to God must be your greater focus. "Submit yourselves therefore to God. Resist the devil, and he will flee from you" (James 4:7).

- *How well are you submitting to God?*
- *Have you aligned yourself in obedience under his will?*
- *Do you persevere in that obedience?*
- *Are you content to stay in that position?*
- *Do you find it a joy to be in submission to God?*

Of course, being arranged under God is a happy experience if it is something that *you* want. You will gladly submit to God when it is his will for you to marry the person you love or to take the job for which you have always dreamed. But submission is really put to the test when it is not your will. D. L. Moody once shared the testimony of a very sick woman. When asked if she wanted to live or die, she responded, "Which God pleases."

"But," said one, "if God should refer it to you, which would you choose?"

She replied, "Truly, I would refer it to him again."

Moody added, "Thus we obtain the will of God when our will is subjected to God."[4] The chorus of an old Gospel song reads:

Oh, to be saved from myself, dear Lord,
Oh, to be lost in Thee;
Oh, that it may be no more I,
But Christ that lives in me.[5]

Perfect submission occurs when your will is so totally aligned with God's will, that yours is lost and only his is seen!

CHAPTER 2 - OBEDIENCE

The first color that breaks forth from our prism when submission is put through it is arrangement, and then obedience quickly follows. That's because a proper arrangement in your life necessitates obedience. Parents instinctively understand this. A mother may say to little Johnny who has been misbehaving, "Johnny, you'd better get in line." She does not mean that he is supposed to stand directly behind her. She is telling him that he must start obeying. Lining up under authority (submission) demands obedience to that authority. What is true for a child's submission to his parents is also true of your submission to God. You must obey him, but instantly you are confronted with a problem.

The Beginning: A Changed Heart

In Romans 8:7, the Scripture says, "Because the carnal mind is enmity against God: for it is not subject [in submission] to the law of God, neither indeed can be." The carnal (fleshly, unsaved) mind is not in submission to the law of God. In fact, it is at enmity with God. This is a state of rebellion. The natural solution that is offered to this problem is that this mind needs to give up its state of rebellion and start obeying God. But ultimately, this is futile because while that individual may obey for a time, in the end, he would fail. Paul declares that the carnal mind is simply not capable of subjecting itself to God's law ("neither indeed can be").

The reason for this futility is illustrated two chapters later in Romans when Paul discusses the Jews' problem. "For they being ignorant of God's righteousness, and going about to establish their own righteousness, have not submitted themselves unto the righteousness of God" (10:3). Paul argued that they were trying to establish their own righteousness (through the keeping of the law), but in so doing, they were not in submission to God's righteousness.

That almost sounds paradoxical until you understand the primary argument in the book of Romans. Romans 1:16-17 reads, "For I am not ashamed of the gospel of Christ: for it is the power of God unto salvation to every one that believeth; to the Jew first, and also to the Greek. For therein is the righteousness of God revealed from faith to faith: as it is written, The just shall live by faith." In other words, the righteousness of God is not attained through good works but through faith in Jesus Christ. He died on the cross for your sins, paying your sin debt, so that when you place your faith in him for salvation, you receive his righteousness. "For he hath made him to be sin for us, who knew no sin; that we might be made the righteousness of God in him" (2 Cor. 5:21). In short, that means you must have a change of heart by receiving the salvation that Christ offers before you will be capable of submitting to God's law.

A Spiritual Act

When you place your faith in Christ, God's Holy Spirit comes to live within you, and he gives you the ability to submit to God by obeying his Word. After stating that the carnal mind cannot submit and obey God, Paul declares, "But ye are not in the flesh, but in the Spirit...and if Christ be in you, the body is dead because of sin; but the Spirit is life because of righteousness" (Rom. 8:9-10).

Since you are now spiritually alive, you are able to walk in the Spirit (Rom. 8:4)—to be arranged in submission under God. This order is important, and the Lord knew it. Christ gave the Great Commission to his disciples before returning to heaven, and in that commission, he told them to be "teaching them to observe all things whatsoever I have commanded you" (Matt. 28:20a). But before they could do that, they must make disciples. Therefore, in order for one to obey the Lord, he must first have made the heart decision to follow the Lord by faith.

Yet, the follower of Christ is one who obeys Christ. Jesus said, "If ye love me, keep my commandments" (John 14:15). And the Apostle John later wrote, "And hereby we do know that we know him, if we keep his commandments" (1 John 2:3).

A Dedicated Body

Obedient submission is more than a *spiritual* act. Since man is made up of a body and a soul, submission must include obedient actions of the *body*. Paul instructs, "Neither yield ye your members as instruments of unrighteousness unto sin: but yield yourselves unto God, as those that are alive from the dead, and your members as instruments of righteousness unto God" (Rom. 6:13). The "members" he is talking about are the various parts of your body. These you must yield to God. The word "yield" can mean "to present, as in a dedication" (cf. Luke 2:22). Paul says that you must present your body unto God as a tool of righteousness. The Lord desires that you give him a dedicated body.

Curiously, Paul uses the same word in Romans 12:1, where he urges you to "present your bodies a living sacrifice, holy, acceptable unto God." As followers of Christ, you and I are to have bodies dedicated to do the will of God. It is easy to agree with that...on the surface. But too many Christians want to name the name of Christ (as if they were submitting to him on a spiritual level) without obeying him with their bodies (the daily, earthly level). It doesn't work that way. Jesus lamented, "And why call ye me, Lord, Lord, and do not the things which I say?" (Luke 6:46).

Submission must begin in the heart (arrangement), but it also must show in daily life (obedience). If you are not obeying God on a daily basis, you are not submitting to him.

The Example of Jonah

When the Lord came to Jonah with his first assignment of bringing good news to King Jeroboam II, Jonah was eager to say, "Yes, Lord" (2 Kings 14:25). That task pleased him. But when God asked him to go to Nineveh and preach against that great city, Jonah refused. *With his body*, he ran in the opposite direction. While on the floundering ship in the middle of the Mediterranean, Jonah professed to be a follower of "the Lord, the God of heaven" (Jon. 1:9), but while Jonah was saying, "Lord, Lord," he was in direct defiance to the will of God. This is not submission. If you are going to claim submission with your mouth, you had better demonstrate it with your life.

Incidentally, Jonah is also a good example of the fact that outward obedience is not sufficient for complete submission. Later in his book, you find that when Jonah did go and preach in Nineveh, his heart was still not right with God (4:1). He was like the little boy who refused to sit down although his mother repeatedly had told him to do so. The boy continued to stand, until finally, his mother plopped him down in a chair. Fuming, the boy muttered, "I may be sitting down on the *outside*, but I am standing up on the *inside!*" Submission is first arrangement—an attitude of getting into one's place. But in that place, you must obey.

How submissive are you? Are you like Jonah—quick to name the Lord as your God but refuse to obey what he says?

- You know what God says about anger, but you don't take any steps to correct your quick temper.
- You know what God says about lust, but you continue to watch those filthy shows on television or look at explicit pictures on your computer.
- You know what God says about gossip, but you make excuses for what you do or convince yourself that it isn't that bad.
- You know what God says about forgiveness, but you refuse to offer it to the one who wronged you.

This double standard could be applied to every sin. I may not have named yours, but there is probably an area in your life in which you find it difficult to submit to God with obedience. It is at that point that your submission is really tested! The test of submission is not when you find God's will to be easy but hard.

When God asked Jonah to deliver his profitable message to Jeroboam, Jonah appeared to be a submissive prophet. That was easy. But the real test of Jonah's submission came when God called him to preach to Nineveh. That's when Jonah's lack of submission became evident.

The Example of Jesus

Read carefully this description about Jesus:

> Who, being in the form of God, thought it not robbery to be equal with God: But made himself of no reputation, and took upon him the form of a servant, and was made in the likeness of men: And being found in fashion as a man, he humbled himself, and **became obedient** unto death, even the death of the cross. (Phil. 2:6-8)

In his body as a man, Jesus submitted in complete obedience to the will of God—even though it took him to the cross. Was it easy for him? Certainly not! Why else would Jesus cry out in his darkest hour, "My God, my God, why hast thou forsaken me?" (Matt. 27:46). But this was the will of God for him. And through his submissive obedience, Jesus was able to fulfill his purpose—to secure our salvation. Hebrews 5:8-9 says, "Though he were a Son, yet learned he obedience by the things which he suffered; And being made perfect, he became the author of eternal salvation unto all them that obey him." Like Christ, you will only fulfill your God-given purpose in life if you are obediently submissive to God.

In 2014, we acquired a service dog for our son to help him with some of his special needs. KaBam is a loveable Golden Retriever, who enjoys eating and playing like any dog. He loves people and has never met a stranger. When people approach, his tail starts wagging because he is confident that they are coming to pet him. But as a service dog, he has been trained to remain in a heel, without reaching for food on the floor and without lunging at people with outstretched hands. He must sit when he is told. He must perform his service to my son when it is necessary. Only when KaBam is submissively obedient is he able to fulfill the work for which he was bred and trained to do.

Many people fear that obedience to God will take away their joy and freedom, but the opposite is true. Obedience is not slavery; it is freedom. My son's service dog understands that. There is nothing that KaBam would rather do than be with his family. He does not want to be left behind when the family is going out. Because he is obedient, he was trained and certified as a service dog with full public access. He is allowed to go anywhere that we go. Obedience is his ticket to joy and freedom. Proverbs 3:17 says of God's wisdom, "Her ways are ways of pleasantness, and all her paths are peace."

Obeying Earthly Authorities

Your obedient submission to God must also include obedience to your earthly authorities. The Bible repeatedly says that obedience to earthly authorities is an act of obedience to God.

- Wives are to submit to their husbands "as unto the Lord" (Eph. 5:22).
- Children are to obey their parents "in the Lord" (Eph. 6:1).
- Slaves are to be obedient to their masters "as unto Christ" (Eph. 6:5).
- Citizens are commanded to submit to every ordinance "for the Lord's sake" (1 Pet. 2:13).

The only time that it is right to disobey your earthly authority is when that authority commands you to do something contrary to God's Word. A good example of that occurs early in the church's history. Peter and the apostles had been commanded by Christ to preach in his name repentance and remission of sins (Luke 24:47), so when the Sanhedrin demanded that they quit preaching in the name of Jesus (Acts 4:18; 5:28), they refused to comply because, as they argued, "We ought to obey God rather than men" (Acts 5:29b).

But if earthly authorities demand obedience in something that you don't like but is not biblically wrong, God expects you to get in line under them because that is the only way you can be in line under him. Peter explains, "Servants, be subject to your masters with all fear; not only to the good and gentle, but also to the froward [crooked or perverse]. For this is thankworthy, if a man for conscience toward God endure grief, suffering wrongfully" (1 Pet. 2:18-19). Here is another instance in which obedient submission is difficult, but it is right. It pleases God, and he honors it.

While I was preparing this chapter, a prayer request came across my desk for the persecuted believers in China. The authorities had forbidden them to preach the Gospel or to talk to media outlets. I thought about those two requirements. What is the biblical response to such demands? I believe that a quick study of the New Testament answers that question. Christians cannot obey a government directive against preaching the Gospel because Christ has commanded it (Mark 16:15). But God has given no directive about talking to news reporters. In that case, I would say that the believers are to submit to their authority—even if they don't like it.

As with submission to God, so it is true with submission to human authorities; the test of your submission is not when you agree but when you disagree. Yet, even then, God calls you to obey.

CHAPTER 3 – SURRENDER

When the Union army under the command of Ulysses S. Grant captured Fort Donelson, the Confederates hoisted a white flag and asked the terms. Grant replied famously, "No terms other than an unconditional and immediate surrender can be accepted," and thus he earned the nickname "Unconditional Surrender Grant." The fort surrendered.[6]

In separating the colors of submission, we find that surrender is the third. Submission is arrangement under another (usually an authority), which necessitates obedience. But if you are like me, you often struggle with obedience. That is why you need surrender.

Why the struggle?

It might help to understand why we struggle with submission, particularly to God. Most of the time, it is simply because we are sinners. We want our own way, so when God tells us to do something differently, we balk. Isaiah described us so accurately when he said, "All we like sheep have gone astray; we have turned every one to his own way" (Isa. 53:6a). The Apostle Paul explained the conflict within: "For the flesh lusteth against the Spirit, and the Spirit against the flesh: and these are contrary the one to the other: so that ye cannot do the things that ye would" (Gal. 5:17). This was something he knew not only from revelation but also personal experience. He testified, "But I see another law in my members, warring against the law of my mind, and bringing me into captivity to the law of sin which is in my members" (Rom. 7:23).

Depending on your own personal background and makeup, you may struggle with obedience to God and authorities more than others do. But the reality is that everyone struggles to obey sometimes because everyone is born with a desire to go his or her own way. You may struggle with submission to God because you imagine that what he asks you to do is not good for you. In that case, you have predetermined what "good" is—according to your own desires—and cannot accept that God's will is better. Hence, you struggle to submit to him.

But every struggle is not a result of your sinful nature. Sometimes you struggle simply because you are human. This was the case of Jesus Christ. Matthew's account of Jesus' agony in the Garden of Gethsemane is very revealing. He writes, "And he took with him Peter and the two sons of Zebedee, and began to be **sorrowful and very heavy**. Then saith he unto them, My soul is **exceeding sorrowful**, even unto death: tarry ye here, and watch with me. And he went a little further, and fell on his face, and prayed, saying, O my Father, if it be possible, let this cup pass from me: nevertheless **not as I will**, but as thou wilt" (26:37-39).

The words Matthew uses are very descriptive. Clearly, Jesus experienced a great emotional burden. The Scripture says that he was "sorrowful," which means "deeply affected with sadness." He also describes the Lord as "very heavy," which can be a state of near depression. Furthermore, he intensifies the description with Jesus' words "exceeding sorrowful."[7]

Why did Jesus feel this way? His prayer reveals the burden. His Father was giving him a cup to drink, and for the moment, Jesus found it difficult to swallow. The cup refers to the cross and all of the suffering (particularly spiritual suffering) that would be involved. But in all of this emotional struggle, Jesus did not sin (1 Pet. 2:21-23). This was not a sinful struggle; it was a human struggle. He was being asked to bear something no other human had ever done or could ever do—to pay for the sins of the world (1 Pet. 2:24) and experience separation from the Father while doing it (Matt. 27:46). His righteous soul, which had always known nothing but full and perfect fellowship with God, recoiled at the bitter cup.

Clearly, Jesus' struggle was quite different from the struggles you usually have with God's will. I imagine that you typically recoil from obeying God because you are sinful not because you are pure. Nevertheless, there are times when you may find yourself struggling to submit to God simply because your flesh is weak. I do not suggest that there is no selfishness and pride mixed in your struggle, but there is something very human about a struggle with such things as martyrdom, deprivation, physical pain, and personal loss.

Even the greatest of saints struggled in such moments. The English Archbishop Thomas Cranmer was used of God in a powerful way to further the Reformation in England, but following the death of Edward VI and the accession of Mary Tudor to the throne, Cranmer faced severe persecution. Through imprisonment and the gradual wearing down by his enemies, Cranmer, in a moment of weakness, signed a paper recanting his protestant beliefs. John Foxe said that it was no doubt "the love of life" that tempted Cranmer to recant, and we, who have never had to face being burned at the stake, cannot fully understand the struggle of his soul. But Cranmer recanted his recantation, which doomed him to the flames. When the fire was lit around him, he thrust his right hand into it first, declaring, "This unworthy right hand."[8]

But whether your struggle is the result of your sinful condition or simply being human, you must discover the surrender in submission.

What if you don't surrender?

If you don't surrender to God, you will experience God's resistance—his opposition. James warns, "God resisteth the proud, but giveth grace unto the humble. Submit yourselves therefore to God"

(James 4:6b-7a). In other words, you will find God to be your enemy, which is not an enviable position.

A perfect illustration of what happens when a man refuses to submit to God is found in the Old Testament during the last days of the Kingdom of Judah. The Babylonians had besieged Jerusalem; some had already defected and went over to the enemy's side. Jeremiah told King Zedekiah that his best course was surrender: "Go out to Nebuchadnezzar, and you and your house will live. But if you refuse this word of the Lord, know that this city will be destroyed."[9] To us, who know the end of the story, surrender looks reasonable, but to Zedekiah, the son of the great King Josiah, surrender seemed foolish. It seemed cowardly. It was contrary to what his officials were telling him. It was not the message that his heart wanted to hear.

Zedekiah refused to submit to God by surrendering to the Babylonians. As a result, God opposed him. In the eleventh year of his reign, the Babylonians broke through the wall of Jerusalem. They burned the city. They captured the king, and before his eyes, they slaughtered his sons. And while that horrid picture was still fresh on his mind, they blinded him, bound him with chains, and carried him off to Babylon to die (Jer. 39:2-7).

The Bible contains a graveyard riddled with men and women who refused to surrender to God and met his opposition. It's not worth it. When God chastens you—whether because of sin or simply to train you in godliness—you need to submit. Resisting the hand of God is *never* for your good.

How do you surrender?

Let us return to Jesus in the Garden for there he demonstrates perfect submission through surrender. The words of Luke are the most helpful in our study at this point. "And he was withdrawn from them about a stone's cast, and kneeled down, and prayed, saying, Father, if thou be **willing**, remove this cup from me: nevertheless not my **will**, but thine, be done" (Luke 22:41-42). There are two "wills" here: the Father's and Christ's. The Greek word that Luke uses for Christ's will ("my will") [10] indicates a choice, even at times a wish. The word he uses for the Father's will ("thou be willing") [11] often implies a deliberate selection. To paraphrase, Jesus says, "Not my choice but your deliberate selection for my life." In short, Jesus submits his will to the Father's will. He recognizes that the Father's will is greater, and he arranges his will under the Father's.

But how did he come to this surrender? In the first place, Jesus prayed. In fact, he prayed three times (Matt. 26:39, 42, 44). By the time the guards came to arrest him, the matter had been settled between God and him. John tells how Peter tried to defend Jesus with the sword but was rebuked of the Lord, "Put up thy sword into the sheath: the cup which my Father hath given me, shall I not drink it?" (John 18:11). The soul will rarely reach the place of surrender apart from prayer. In fact, sometimes it is necessary to pray multiple times, every time dragging the unwilling soul back to the altar of surrender.

But prayer was not the only foundation for Jesus' surrender. Matthew also records how Peter drew his sword in an attempt to defend Jesus (though he does not name Peter). He provides the rest of Jesus' statement to Peter that night. Not only had Christ said that he must drink the cup (John 18:11), but he also said that he knew this is what he must do because "the scriptures [must] be fulfilled" (Matt. 26:54). In other words, Jesus was relying upon God's Word, which had stated plainly that a perfect sacrifice was necessary in order to redeem mankind from his sins. He knew that he must be that sacrifice!

Jesus lined up his will under the Father's will with the help of prayer and God's Word. On that dark night in Gethsemane, your Savior not only won the victory and found full surrender so that you could be redeemed, but he also showed you the way in which you too can find submissive surrender to God.

When you find yourself struggling with submission, go to the Word of God.

- What does God say you should do?
- What does God promise he will do if you obey?
- What does God say are the consequences for disobedience?
- What do you know from the Bible about God's character that might help you surrender (e.g., God keeps his promises.)?

After you have absorbed that Scripture, go to God in prayer.

- Tell him of your struggle.
- Tell him what you learned in his Word.
- Tell him you want not your own desires for your life but his deliberate choices.

It is the natural instinct of dogs to run in packs, and within those packs, there is a definite hierarchy. One dog is chief, and all the other dogs are expected to submit to him. It is said that when a dog gets into a fight with another dog and realizes that it cannot win, it lies down on the ground baring its neck to its opponent. While this act of submission makes the weaker dog extremely vulnerable, it actually spares its life. God desires your submission. If you are struggling to give it to him in a certain area of your life, then you must come to the place of surrender.

CHAPTER 4 – TRUST

Surrender, especially in war, is usually achieved when a fight makes it evident to one party that it is defeated and has no other recourse. This is a *forced surrender.* It is usually reluctant, such as an army that holds out until it is almost decimated. The result is often bitter, such as the way defeated nations hate the occupying nations. But on occasion, there is a *willing surrender,* which occurs with no fight at all. By his own willing choice, without reluctance or resentment, one party yields to the other. This is the type of submission that God desires from us.

But how can I get to the place of willing surrender? After all, the reason I must *surrender* in the first place is that I am struggling to obey God. The answer is found in TRUST, which is needed for you and me to come to full peaceful surrender to God.

The Link between Submission and Trust

In describing the submission of wives to their husbands, Peter appeals to the Old Testament saints. He writes, "For after this manner in the old time the holy women also, who **trusted** in God, adorned themselves, being in **subjection** unto their own husbands" (1 Pet. 3:5). This verse demonstrates that there is a link between submission and trust. Of course, I realize that the submission of the wives here is to their husbands, and their trust is in God; but as has already been mentioned, if a wife is not properly arranged under her husband, she is not properly arranged under God. So there is an indirect reference to her submission to God.

The second psalm is a Messianic psalm talking about Christ's final victory over his enemies (cf. Rev. 2:27). David begins by describing the heathen rulers raging and rebelling against Christ. They think that they can fight against him (rather than surrender). But David says that God just sits in the heavens and laughs at them because he has set Jesus Christ on the throne, and he will be victorious. Someday, he will break the heathen and dash them in pieces. David's conclusion is pointed: "Kiss the Son, lest he be angry, and ye perish from the way, when his wrath is kindled but a little. Blessed are all they that put their trust in him" (Ps. 2:12). In the ancient world, you showed submission and subservience to a monarch by bowing down before him and kissing him (on his feet, hand, ring, etc.).[12]

The crucial application of the psalm is that you must submit to Christ or suffer judgment. Only in Christ is salvation (Acts 4:12). But notice the last phrase: "Blessed are all they that put their **trust** in him." Here's that link again between submission and trust. To surrender to Jesus Christ and submit to him is an act of faith (trust).

Until you settle the matter in your heart that you can trust God no matter what happens, you will always struggle to surrender to him, especially if you perceive his will to be something difficult. The question then is: *Will you trust God?*

Example of Jesus

Jesus is the perfect example of submission to God. Peter says of him, "Who, when he was reviled, reviled not again; when he suffered, he threatened not; but **committed** himself to him that judgeth righteously" (1 Pet. 2:23). Jesus was maligned and falsely accused. He was dragged before Pilate, who was far from a righteous judge. But Jesus submitted to God's will—a will that he knew involved the cross and, therefore, all the abuse preceding it. Jesus' surrender is illustrated in the Garden of Gethsemane, but in Pilate's hall, his trust in God is displayed.

The word "committed" means "to give into the hands of." The Jews had delivered (same word) Christ to Pontius Pilate (Matt. 27:2), but Jesus delivered himself into God's hands. "Jesus answered [Pilate], Thou couldest have no power at all against me, except it were given thee from above: therefore he that delivered me unto thee hath the greater sin" (John 19:11). He knew the evil had come upon him according to God's will; he trusted God and was therefore able to submit.

How do you submit to an authority who is unkind or evil?

That was one of the great questions that Peter took up in his first epistle. He wrote to a group of suffering Christians, "Wherefore let them that suffer according to the will of God commit the keeping of their souls to him in well doing, as unto a faithful Creator" (1 Pet. 4:19). You can submit to an unkind or evil authority when you learn to trust God. Sometimes submission to our authorities results in suffering, and some suffering is within the will of God. But in any case, you must put your trust in God—not in man. Psalm 118:8 declares, "It is better to trust in the LORD than to put confidence in man." Proverbs 29:25 reminds us, "The fear of man bringeth a snare: but whoso putteth his trust in the LORD shall be safe."

In 1 Peter 3, the apostle provides specific instructions for wives with unsaved husbands. They are called to submit to their husbands, but that isn't always easy. Even if an unsaved man doesn't ask his wife to do anything sinful, sometimes he is difficult to get along with. What should she do? Verse 5 says, "Trust in the Lord." This is the secret! No matter what circumstances may come into your life, no matter what people may do, God is still in control. He is over all, and he can be trusted!

This is what Jesus understood when, before Pilate, he fully submitted to suffering in the will of God. He didn't trust the Jews. He didn't trust Pilate. He didn't trust Roman or Jewish law. He trusted God. But sometimes our trust in God is weak.

Example of Abraham

Abraham's sacrifice of Isaac is a beautiful illustration of submissive obedience that springs from surrender and trust. God told Abraham to sacrifice Isaac on a mountain in Moriah, and Abraham obeyed. In fact, he wasted no time in obeying for Moses records, "And Abraham rose up early in the morning" (Gen. 22:1-3).

The passage says very little of Abraham's emotions; it does not say if there was a great struggle in his heart. But what loving father wouldn't struggle with God's request to sacrifice his son? Actually, I believe that the Scripture subtly describes Abraham's struggle. For example, God himself acknowledged that Isaac was "thy son, thine only son Isaac, whom thou lovest" (v. 2). Such a redundant description emphasizes first that Isaac was the son of promise—the son God had promised to give Abraham and to make into a great nation. That promise and this command seemed to contradict each other. Surely, that contradiction would have created some confusion in the patriarch's mind. Second, God's description of Isaac admits that the boy was dearly loved by his father. In fact, that's the crux of the test: does Abraham love Isaac or God more?

As one reads the account of the events leading up to Isaac's sacrifice, one gets the distinct impression that Moses is portraying the heavy heart of Abraham. He accomplishes this by describing such mundane details as rising early in the morning, saddling the donkey, splitting the wood, and leaving the servants behind. In addition, Abraham's words seem to be few (vv. 5-9). Clearly, he hadn't told anyone what he was going to do, not even Isaac (v. 7). Moses seems to indicate that they journeyed with relative silence. I imagine Abraham was extremely solemn and deep in thought.

But in spite of this struggle, he surrenders and obeys God. The Scripture implies that he would have gone through with the act if God had not stopped him when it says, "[he] took the knife to slay his son" (v. 10).

This is truly a remarkable act, especially when you consider that a number of years earlier, Abraham struggled to obey a much easier command: to wait for the son of promise. In that case, he heeded his wife's suggestion to go in to Hagar and have a son by her (Gen. 16:2). But much had transpired since that time, and Abraham had learned better how to submit to God. What was his secret? TRUST.

Abraham had a stronger faith in Genesis 22 than in Genesis 16. He had come to the point where he knew he could trust God no matter what. There's no question that Abraham had faith those many years before (Gen. 15:6), but that faith was not strong enough to enable him to submit in waiting. Years later, when God put him to the greatest test of his life, Abraham's faith did not waver. He said to the servants, "I and the lad will go yonder and worship, **and come again to you**" (22:5). He told Isaac, "**God will provide** himself a lamb for a burnt offering" (22:8). The writer of Hebrews brings out this faith with force (Heb. 11:17-19).

During those intervening years, Abraham had grown in his faith. He had come to *know* God better; therefore, he had come to *trust* God better. And herein is the secret of surrender: the better you know God, the better you will trust him.

When you learn to trust, you willingly surrender in submission to God because you know that God's understanding of the situation is far better than your own. Yet, that knowledge is not enough because trust must engage more than the mind. It must get to the heart. Therefore, you must surrender in submission to God because you have a heart relationship with God (Prov. 3:5). You have given him all your heart and have found him to be fully trustworthy and good.

For this reason, Abraham had no trouble in trusting God on top of Moriah and was willing to submit in what must have been the most agonizing test he ever faced. During the years since God had promised him a multitude of descendants under a starry sky, Abraham had come to know God intimately. No wonder he was so confident while ascending Mount Moriah that his God was *Jehovah-Jireh* (Gen. 22:14).[13]

Submission to God requires a trust in God—a trust that is rooted in an intimate relationship with him. Only in that position are you able to surrender peacefully.

I had been going through a difficult time in my ministry. The trials were various, but the greatest was an inner turmoil, in which I found myself struggling to accept what God was doing in my ministry. While this battle raged within, I began meditating on Jesus Christ, particularly how he had set his face as a flint to go up to Jerusalem knowing that he was going to be arrested and crucified (Luke 9:51). Yet, he refused to waver because he had committed his soul to God, the One who judges righteously (1 Pet. 2:23).

A sermon based on that theme began to develop in my mind, and then a poem took form in my head. Diligently I worked on the words and handed them to my wife. "I'd like you to make this into a song for Sunday," I announced to her on Thursday evening. I have sprung such projects on her before, but it always flusters her when I put her under a time constraint. But as she had done so many times before, she rose to the occasion and created a beautiful tune to match my words. By the time we had gone to bed on Friday night, the song sat finished on our piano. I intended to sing it after my sermon on Sunday.

But it was not meant to be…at least not that week. In the early morning hours on Saturday, a flash flood tore through our valley. I awoke around 2 a.m., walked out into the kitchen, and stepped into water. In a space of four hours, the creek behind our house rose more than eight feet. The house was surrounded. The crawl space was full of water. Our church next door was flooded. In the morning, I surveyed the damage; it left me bewildered.

Naturally, there were no church services on the Sunday for which I had been planning. That day, like all the others that followed in the week, was spent in cleanup. Physically, I was exhausted. Emotionally, I felt like giving up. But God took the words of our newly written song and sang them over and over to my troubled heart. I was reminded that no matter what happens, I can trust the Lord.

I Can Trust the Lord
When the future is unknown to me,
I can trust the Lord.
When the way before I cannot see,
I can trust the Lord.
When my feelings are in turmoil
And my heart can find no rest,
Jesus is my great example,
Trusting God in every test.

Chorus:
He set his face as a flint towards Jerusalem.
He drank with joy the cup that his Father gave.
He died alone, while the crowds were mocking and jeering.
But with every step, Jesus trusted the Lord.

Since the promises of God are true,
I can trust the Lord.
Since his grace will give me strength anew,
I can trust the Lord.
Since his love is ever certain
In the heights or in the depths,
Looking only unto Jesus,
I will follow in his steps.

Chorus:
He set his face as a flint towards Jerusalem.
He drank with joy the cup that his Father gave.
He died alone, while the crowds were mocking and jeering.
But with every step, Jesus trusted the Lord.

CHAPTER 5 – HUMILITY

There will be no true submission without humility. The reason for that is found in the basic meaning of the word. Submission is arrangement—arranging yourself *under* another. That doesn't happen unless you humble yourself. But there is also a biblical connection between humility and submission.

The Biblical Connection

James writes,

> But he giveth more grace. Wherefore he saith, God resisteth the proud, but giveth grace unto the humble. Submit yourselves therefore to God. Resist the devil, and he will flee from you. Draw nigh to God, and he will draw nigh to you. Cleanse your hands, ye sinners; and purify your hearts, ye double minded. Be afflicted, and mourn, and weep: let your laughter be turned to mourning, and your joy to heaviness. Humble yourselves in the sight of the Lord, and he shall lift you up (James 4:6-10).

It is important to note the "therefore" in verse 7. It points back to the necessity of humility in verse 6. Because God gives grace only to the humble, you need to submit to him. In James's mind, humility before God and submission to him go hand in hand, and that is borne out in what follows. After giving his simple statement of submission in the first half of verse 7, James provides an explanation of how it should unfold in your life, especially as it concerns the removal of sin and worldliness from your heart (vv. 3-5). James presents it in a series of couplets.

> *Submit yourselves therefore to God. (v. 7a)*
>
> *Resist the devil. (v. 7b)*
> *Draw nigh to God. (v. 8a)*
>
> *Cleanse your hands. (v. 8b)*
> *Purify your hearts. (v. 8c)*
>
> *Be afflicted, and mourn. (v. 9a)*
> *Let your laughter be turned to mourning. (v. 9b)*
>
> *Humble yourselves in the sight of the Lord. (v. 10)*

As you can see from the basic diagram above, the second phrase of the couplet for "submit yourselves" (v. 7) does not come until verse 10 ("Humble yourselves"). Thus, James creates a "sandwich effect" for the entire passage. Humility is an expression of submission.

Peter also demonstrates this connection when he writes, "Likewise, ye younger, **submit** yourselves unto the elder. Yea, all of you be subject one to another, and be clothed with **humility**: for God resisteth the proud, and giveth grace to the humble. Humble yourselves therefore under the mighty hand of God, that he may exalt you in due time" (1 Pet. 5:5-6). The younger are called to arrange themselves under the older. While this is not an arrangement based upon authority, it does require humility, which is why Peter emphasizes it. Then he quotes the same Old Testament passage that James quoted (Prov. 3:34) and adds the command that you ought to humble yourself before God. There is no true submission without humility.

The Son's Example

Once again, Jesus Christ is the perfect example of submission, vividly reflecting the color of humility. In describing Christ's submission, the Apostle Paul states, "And being found in fashion as a man, **he humbled himself**, and became obedient unto death, even the death of the cross" (Phil. 2:8). Jesus himself testified that he had come to serve (Luke 22:27).

In his classic work, *Humility*, Andrew Murray keenly brings out Jesus' humble relationship with the Father. Here is his list of verses with emphases: [14]

> "The Son can **do nothing of himself**, but what he seeth the Father do" (John 5:19).

> "I can of mine own self **do nothing**" (John 5:30).

> "For I came down from heaven, **not to do mine own will**, but the will of him that sent me" (John 6:38).

> "My doctrine is **not mine**, but his that sent me" (John 7:16).

> "I am **not come of myself**, but he that sent me is true, whom ye know not" (John 7:28).

> "When ye have lifted up the Son of man, then shall ye know that I am he, and that **I do nothing of myself**; but as my Father hath taught me, I speak these things" (John 8:28).

> "I proceeded forth and came from God; **neither came I of myself**, but he sent me" (John 8:42).

> "And I seek **not mine own glory**: there is one that seeketh and judgeth" (John 8:50).

> "The words that I speak unto you **I speak not of myself**: but the Father that dwelleth in me, he doeth the works" (John 14:10).

> "The word which ye hear is **not mine**, but the Father's which sent me" (John 14:24).

Murray writes, "Christ was nothing, that God might be all. He resigned himself with his will and his powers entirely for the Father to work in him....His humility was simply the surrender of himself to God, to allow the Father to do in him what he pleased."[15] Jesus' submission to God was characterized by utter humility. Only God and God's will mattered in his life, which is why he ultimately was able to pray in the Garden, "Not my will but thine be done."

The Disciple's Lifestyle

Jesus urged his disciples to follow his humble submission. While in the Upper Room, he said to them, "Verily, verily, I say unto you, The servant is not greater than his lord; neither he that is sent greater than he that sent him" (John 13:16). For three and a half years, these men had observed Jesus in perfect humble submission to the Father. But on this particular night, these words came with a powerful force.

Jesus knew that his hour had come—that is, that he would soon be betrayed, arrested, and crucified. John records that Jesus also knew that the Father had given all things into his hands (13:3). Everything was to be put under the feet of Jesus Christ. In other words, everything (including his disciples) was to get in line under Christ. That's submission. But this same Jesus rose from supper, laid aside his garments, and girded himself with a towel. In this attire, he appeared as a slave. Then he proceeded to wash the feet of each of the disciples. Here is the Son of God to whom everything has been given, kneeling down on the ground washing dirty feet! Why? According to Jesus' own words, it was to teach the disciples by example that their lifestyle must be characterized by submissive humility (vv. 12-15)—not just to God but to one another.

Paul understood this connection when just prior to that beautiful description of the submissive humility of Jesus Christ (Phil. 2:6-8), he urges, "Let this mind be in you, which was also in Christ Jesus." And such an attitude will affect our relationships with one another. He declared, "Let nothing be done through strife or vainglory [self-conceit]; but in lowliness of mind let each esteem other better than themselves. Look not every man on his own things, but every man also on the things of others" (Phil. 2:3-4).

Surely, this was also in the back of James's mind when he urged his readers to humble themselves before God and submit to him. His words followed his pointed exhortations about interpersonal relationships (4:1-2). James nails the problem right on the head when he answers the question, "Why do you have conflicts with other people?" His answer cuts to the quick: you have interpersonal conflicts because they spring from your "lusts" (i.e., your desires and personal ambitions). The problem is that you want *your* way; you don't want to submit. Simply put, you are *selfish*.

Selfishness is at the heart of nearly every sibling fight. Johnny wants the toy that Tommy had, but the moment he picks it up, Tommy decides he wants to play with it again. A tug-of-war match ensues, which often ends in a brawl or tears. Then, the parent steps in, stops the fight, and gives a brief lecture on sharing. But ultimately, the problem is that both children are being selfish. Each wants his own way, and neither will submit to the other.

It would be wonderful if children grew out of selfishness just as they grow out of their childish toys, but they don't. As an adult, I still struggle with wanting my own way, and I'm sure you do, too. It shows up in your irritation when the cashier rings up your order wrong and sends you over to customer service to get it fixed, where you must wait in another slow-moving line. It shows up at church when others don't see it your way, and you find yourself fuming on the inside. It shows up when your spouse asks you to change some behavior, but your thought is only how that will cramp your style. In each case, you struggle to submit to another because you are selfish.

But this is not the way Jesus lived. Not only did he submit to God in humility, but he was also willing to submit to others because of that humility. His was a humility that permeated his whole life. Christ was not selfish; he was *selfless*. Andrew Murray observed, "Because Christ had thus humbled himself before God, and God was ever before him, he found it possible to humble himself before men, too. He was able to be the Servant of all. His humility was simply the surrender of himself to God, to allow the Father to do in him what he pleased, no matter what men around might say of him, or do to him."[16]

In short, if you have trouble getting along with other people, the real problem is not *them* or the *issue*. The real problem is in your heart; it is an unwillingness to surrender your rights, your desires, or your praise. Out of humility, submission says, "I will yield." Of course, you must understand that this is not about doing anything wrong—yielding your biblical convictions in order to sin because someone insists on it. This is about yielding your *personal* wishes. That's tough because we're usually more like the disciples than Jesus. We're more willing to sit around and talk about who is going to be the greatest and complain about everyone else's dirty feet than we are to get up, lay aside our comforts, and stoop to wash those feet, including the feet of our enemies. Remember, Jesus washed Judas's feet that night, too!

John MacArthur describes a young man who had concluded that God wanted him to be a missionary. MacArthur explains, "But our young friend, despite his dedication, has some problems. He is a little headstrong. He seems to have trouble getting along with those in authority over him. His reasons for rebellion are very good, of course, at least in his eyes." Finally, seeking the counsel of his pastor, he says, "I believe God wants me to be a missionary, but I'm not sure whether he wants me to be a home missionary or a foreign missionary." The wise old man peers at him for a moment and says, "Young man, what you need to be first of all is a 'submissionary.' You need to learn what submission means."[17]

If you have trouble getting along with people, you have a problem with submission, and that's because you have a problem with humility. Jesus said, "Verily, verily, I say unto you, The servant is not greater than his lord; neither he that is sent greater than he that sent him" (John 13:16). Jesus urged this attitude of his disciples *after* he washed their feet as an example of humility, and *before* his greatest surrender (in the Garden) and his greatest act of submission (the Cross). You will not come to the surrender of obedient submission unless you choose humility before God and men.

God's will for your life isn't always easy to accept. That health problem, family crisis, child's future, or job situation is not working out the way you planned. If you find yourself struggling to submit to God's will, not only do you need to learn how to trust God better (recognizing that he's not going to ask you to do something that is not good for you), but you also need to learn more humility. Bow the knee. God is greater. He has the right to do as he pleases. Resign your desires, and accept his will.

Murray makes this powerful observation: "[Jesus Christ] lost nothing by giving everything to God. The Father honored his trust and did all for him, and then exalted him to his own right hand in glory."[18] You and I need Peter's advice: "Humble yourselves therefore under the mighty hand of God, that he may exalt you in due time" (1 Pet. 5:6).

CHAPTER 6 – REVERENCE

You can surrender to someone that you do not love. It happens in war all the time. You can humble yourself before someone that you do not respect. That often happens when your opponent beats you. But it is difficult to trust someone that you do not respect. Thus, if your surrender is going to be done willingly and if it is going to be based upon trust, there must be reverence, especially for God.

Reverence and Submission in Relationships

The Bible requires submission in at least seven different relationships. Three of them specifically link reverence (respect) with that submission.

Children to parents

The Scriptures teach that children are to be in subjection to their parents by obeying them (Eph. 6:1). Such was the example of Jesus in his youth (Luke 2:51). And the writer of Hebrews assumes the submission of children to their parents when he likens the discipline of earthly fathers to that of the Heavenly Father. Yet, he also points out that such submission involves reverence. Hebrews 12:9 states, "Furthermore we have had fathers of our flesh which corrected us, and we gave them reverence: shall we not much rather be in subjection [submission] unto the Father of spirits, and live?"

When I was growing up, I had a healthy fear of my father and grandfather. I would have much sooner borne the wrath of my mother than my father. Permit me to clarify: neither my father nor my grandfather was abusive, but I certainly didn't wish to upset them. I submitted to their commands in part because I reverenced them and feared what would happen if I disobeyed.

Slaves to masters

The submission of slaves to their masters included respect. Peter wrote to them, "Servants, be subject to your masters with all fear; not only to the good and gentle, but also to the froward [cruel or harsh]" (1 Pet. 2:18). The word "fear" must include the idea of reverence or respect because Peter included the good and gentle masters. Slaves who had gentle masters surely didn't have a reason to be terrified of them, but they did owe them respect.

Paul wrote to Titus, "Exhort servants to be obedient unto their own masters, and to please them well in all things; not answering again" (Titus 2:9). This verse does not include the words "fear" or "reverence," but the concept is there. Slaves were to "be obedient" (literally, "submit") to their masters and to do it in such a way as to please them, which would be the fruit of respectful submission.

Wives to husbands

When Paul discusses marriage roles, he keeps things simple. Husbands are to lead their wives in love (Eph. 5:25). Wives are to submit to their husbands (5:22). But before he concludes his instructions about marriage, Paul emphasizes that a wife's submission does not proceed from a heart of contempt but of respect. He says, "The wife see that she reverence her husband" (5:33b). A wife who truly respects her husband has little trouble submitting to him.

Peter provides Sarah as a fitting example. "For after this manner in the old time the holy women also, who trusted in God, adorned themselves, being in subjection unto their own husbands: even as Sara obeyed Abraham, **calling him lord**." The incident that Peter is referring to is from Genesis 18, where Sarah referred to Abraham as "my lord" while speaking to herself behind the tent door. These were not words of pretense meant to impress her husband or the visiting angels because they were not spoken to anyone but herself. Clearly, Sarah possessed a submission to her husband that flowed out of a heart of utmost respect for him.

Extended to Other Relationships

Although the New Testament does not always bring the *words* "submission" and "respect" together in discussing relationships, a careful study will reveal that the *ideas* are joined. For example, consider the submission of soldiers to superiors. The soldier desires to please his commanding officer, and this desire flows out of a respect for his superior (cf. 2 Tim. 2:4).

Likewise, there must be respect in the submission of younger people to older people (1 Pet. 5:5). As has already been noted, this particular submission requires humility, but it certainly includes respect, too. In fact, the Bible puts a premium on the respect that young people are to show to their elders (Lev. 19:32).

Finally, the attitudes of humility and respect are wrapped up together in the way you treat others. You will never submit to another believer (Eph. 5:21) if you do not have a proper respect for that man or woman. Romans 12:10 admonishes, "Be kindly affectioned one to another with brotherly love; in honor preferring one another." This respect for one another says, "I will prefer you over myself; I will submit to your desires."

Such an attitude must spring from a proper understanding of equality in Christ (Gal. 3:26-28). In this world, everyone is different. Some are born Jews; some are born Gentiles. Some are born slaves; some are born free. Some are men; some are women. But in the spiritual realm and in eternity, these distinctions are erased. Therefore, no one is better than another. You ought to be willing to submit to one another out of respect for whom he or she is in Christ.

Your Submission to God

Your submission to God is the most important of all relationships involving submission. While there are times that it is difficult to respect certain people because of how they act or what they stand for, this is never the case with God. He is perfectly holy and worthy of all honor and respect (Rev. 4:11). The lessons in these human relationships can be rightly applied to your submission to God.

You must acknowledge God's rightful place.

As with humility, you must come to the realization that God is God, and that he has the right to be the Sovereign in your life. If you are expected to submit to your earthly authorities, how much more are you to submit to God's authority. This reality is the essence of the first commandment: "Thou shalt have no other gods before me" (Exod. 20:3). As the supreme authority, he must receive first place. John the Baptist understood this importance when he said of Christ, "He must increase, but I must decrease" (John 3:30).

Do you acknowledge God's rightful place in your life? Many people say they do, but their actions indicate otherwise. Consider the following. Does God have his rightful place in your...

- *Time*—How much time did you spend with God today in reading your Bible and praying?
- *Money*—Do you honor God with the first fruits of your increase (Prov. 3:9), or do you take care of your needs first before giving to the Lord?
- *Worship*—On Sundays, are you found in church? When you go to church, is your mind somewhere else, or do you worship him in spirit and sincerity?
- *Children*—What is your goal in raising your children? Is it for your pleasure, to fulfill your dreams, to take care of you in old age, or to love and serve God above all else? I think that many parents would say it is the last of those goals, but

when you look at the things they allow their children to do or the way in which they treat them, you realize that they have not acknowledged God's rightful place in the rearing of their children.

You must accept God's decisions for your life.

Children and slaves are commanded to submit respectfully, accepting the decisions of their superiors. The Bible acknowledges that sometimes authorities are in the wrong. Some masters are "froward" (i.e., crooked or perverse, 1 Pet. 2:18). Some parents discipline their children "after their own pleasure" (in whatever way seems good to them, whether or not it is best for their children). But neither of these things can be said of God. He disciplines us "for our profit, that we might be partakers of his holiness" (Heb. 12:10).

If you are to accept the decisions of authorities that are sometimes wrong or whose motives are less than ideal, how much more should you accept God's decisions in your life. Yet, this is probably one of the most difficult aspects of submission, especially when God's decisions are contrary to your own personal desires. For example, many Christians struggle to accept God's decision when it involves sickness, a family crisis, a tragic loss, or an unwanted job.

When Joni Eareckson broke her neck and became a quadriplegic through a diving accident, she struggled to accept God's will for her life. One day while talking with a Christian friend from high school, she shot this question at him: "Tell me, do you think God had anything to do with my breaking my neck?" Her friend, Steve, didn't take the question lightly, but he didn't offer her empty comfort either. He went straight to the heart of the matter: "God put you in that chair, Joni. I don't know why, but if you'll trust him instead of fighting him, you'll find out why—if not in this life, then in the next. He let you break your neck because he loves you."[19] I can't imagine very many in the evangelical church today offering such a sound theological answer. Connecting God's will with a tragic accident or God's love with an undesirable circumstance is foreign to many believers today, and that may be one reason why so many Christians struggle in their submission to God.

You must desire God's pleasure in your life.

If slaves are expected to seek the pleasure of their masters through their submissive obedience, how much more should you, a servant of the King of kings, desire to please God in your life (1 Thess. 4:1). This is the pinnacle of your reverence. It begins with your acknowledgement of his rightful place. Then it accepts his decision for your life. Finally, it chooses to do his bidding because it desires to please him. It is in this final step that reverence and love merge into one unified impetus bringing submissive surrender to God's will.

As stated earlier, the first commandment acknowledges God's place, but Jesus understood that proper respect for God flows out of something much greater: love. When asked which of all the commands was the greatest, without hesitating, Jesus quoted Deuteronomy 6:5, "And thou shalt love the Lord thy God with all thine heart, and with all thy soul, and with all thy might" (cf. Matt. 22:36-38).

The Example of Jesus

On the last night with his disciples, Jesus prayed with them. In the first part of his prayer, which is recorded in John 17, Jesus prayed for himself. Considering that this prayer was offered just hours before his arrest and gruesome crucifixion, you might have expected that Jesus' prayer for himself would have been to ask for strength to endure or victory over his enemies. But this was not the subject of his prayer. Rather, he prayed that the Father would glorify him so that he could glorify the Father through his death. In other words, Jesus' prayer for glory involved the cross.

In his commentary, Leon Morris observes, "Since his glorification is to be seen in the cross, it is a prayer rather that the Father's will may be done in him....There is no self-seeking in it."[20] Here is the perfect example of submission that springs out of reverence.

- He acknowledged God's glory as the most important.
- He accepted God's will for his life even though it meant the cross.
- He longed above all else to please his Father through obedience. Earlier, he had declared, "I do always those things that please him" (John 8:29).

Maybe you are finding it difficult to submit to God in some area. Possibly, you are chafing under his will, or you are running from it. You keep saying, "I don't want that. I can't see how that is good. It doesn't fit within my plans." If so, you need to follow the example of your Lord. The surrender of submission can be yours as you learn to trust God, humble yourself before him, and reverence him for who he is.

CHAPTER 7 – PERSEVERANCE

So you have come to the place of surrender in order to obey God submissively. You think the battle is won, but then reality sets in. Surrendering was only the first part in arriving at obedient submission. After that act, there's life! Your submission must be lived out day after day. That's why submissive surrender must be followed with perseverance.

Relationship of Perseverance to Submission

Naturally, some applications of submission may not require perseverance. These are usually the one-time acts.

- Submitting to the government by paying one's taxes
- Submitting to another believer by letting him have his preference
- Submitting to God by fulfilling that task about which he has been prompting you

But then there are those matters in which submission will stretch over an extended time.

- Submitting to God's will in a health problem
- Submitting in obedience by turning from a sin
- Submitting in a long-term difficult relationship

In such cases, perseverance must follow submission because without it, you will not remain in the place of submission. Even the meaning of the words hint at this. I've already noted that the word "submit" means "to arrange under." The New Testament word for "perseverance" is "endurance,"[21] meaning literally, "to remain under." Therefore, it should not be a surprise that perseverance is a facet of submission. Aligning under must often be followed by remaining under. The choice to submit—even if it has finally been won through sincere trust, humility, and reverence—must be followed with perseverance, or the submission will not last.

Example of Jesus

As noted in chapter 3, Jesus won the victory in Gethsemane by surrendering through prayer and meditation on God's Word. But his submissive surrender was followed by perseverance. The writer of Hebrews says that Jesus endured the cross (Heb. 12:2). In other words, he persevered in the submissive act until he saw it through to completion (John 19:30). He refused to be undeterred in accomplishing God's will.

Think of what he endured to purchase your redemption:
- He was lied about during his trials.
- He was slapped, spit upon, and had his beard plucked out.
- He was paraded back and forth from trial to trial all night.
- He was beaten by the Romans with a cat-o'-nine-tails.
- He had a crown of thorns pounded on his head.
- He was nailed to a cross, where he hung in tremendous agony for up to six hours.
- Finally, he had all the sins of the world placed upon him, causing the Father to turn his back upon his beloved Son.

In describing the sufferings of Christ, Peter says, "For even hereunto were ye called: because Christ also suffered for us, leaving us an example, that ye should follow his steps" (1 Pet. 2:21). His example, which you are to follow, includes his submissive perseverance.

Areas of Application

Let's consider three of the most difficult areas in which perseverance is necessary in submission. Each of these is a matter of obedience, but there are different nuances in the endurance required.

A Difficult task

As a soldier in the Lord's army, you must submit to God, obeying the orders he gives you. But sometimes those orders are difficult. You may be called to be a missionary in a difficult field. You may be called to take on a new ministry at church—one that pushes you out of your comfort zone. You may be called to witness to your neighbor next door, who has previously made it clear that he wants nothing to do with religion. Such difficult tasks require submission.

But following your surrender to obey, there must be perseverance. The missionary's job isn't done in a day; it's a life-long calling. If you are going to be effective in your new ministry, you can't quit after the second week. And rarely will a person be saved upon hearing the Gospel the first time. Your submission requires perseverance, especially when the task is difficult.

Paul testified, "Wherein I suffer trouble, as an evil doer, even unto bonds; but the word of God is not bound. Therefore I endure all things for the elect's sakes" (2 Tim. 2:9-10a). Previously, Paul had urged Timothy to "endure hardness as a good soldier of Jesus Christ" (2:2), but he didn't require anything of Timothy that he himself wasn't doing. He had been given the task of being the Apostle to the Gentiles, and it had been fraught with trouble and persecution. But Paul endured it all. In fact, as he concluded his last letter, he declared, "I have fought a good fight, I have finished my course, I have kept the faith" (2 Tim. 4:7). That's endurance!

An Overwhelming Trial

James provides counsel for the various trials believers may face. He says, "My brethren, count it all joy when ye fall into divers temptations" (James 1:2). The word "fall" infers a fall into something that surrounds or overwhelms you. James's picture is not a stumble but a complete engulfing by a trial. I think that is a perfect description for the way many of life's trials are. Most of us can take the little problems in stride. It's the overwhelming ones that we find hard to bear—the ones in which we struggle to submit. Often, these trials are not over in a day, a week, or a month. Sometimes they last for years! I'm referring to trials such as sickness, marital problems, a rebellious child, the slander of a former friend, or the time-consuming rebuilding following certain natural disasters.

My wife and I were engulfed in one of those overwhelming trials when we were in Russia adopting our son. Three days into our trip, our home caught fire and burned to the ground. I will never forget the moment when my mother broke the shocking news to me over an international telephone call. Financial concerns quickly flooded my mind. I had no idea how we were going to rebuild our lives and repay all that we had borrowed for an international adoption. Feeling somewhat numb from the news, I sat down and opened my Bible to Psalms, looking for comfort. I was so stunned that I could barely think, but the Lord directed me to Psalm 145. The words of David ministered to my soul. "The LORD upholdeth all that fall, and raiseth up all those that be bowed down" (v. 14).

With a renewed trust in the Lord, we decided to persevere in what we believed God had led us to do: to adopt a baby boy. Returning home, we learned of the tremendous generosity of God's people. The Lord used our house fire not only to give us a new home but also to pay for our son's adoption in full. But we soon had a new burden. I had to oversee the rebuilding phase, including the endless insurance paperwork. This was in addition to my regular ministry responsibilities. And I was trying to adjust to the care of an infant son. A fire or flood can destroy everything in a matter of hours, but it takes months before a state of normalcy returns to your life. That requires perseverance.

Whatever the trial, James tells us to count it pure joy. Of course, that seems absurd to our thinking. Our first response is usually something like, "Why me?" or "How am I going to get through this?" James's counsel is rooted in the call to submission. You and I must learn to say, "Lord, I accept this trial as from your hand. I know you have a plan for my good and your glory through this." Yet, even when you reach that point of submission, it will take perseverance to stay there.

James continues, "Knowing this, that the trying of your faith worketh patience. But let patience have her perfect work, that ye may be perfect [mature] and entire, wanting [lacking] nothing" (1:3-4). The word "trying" describes the process of putting something to the test to find out what it's made of. When your faith is put to the test in trials, not only do you find out what it is made of, but also a by-product is formed in your life: endurance. And that is a necessary ingredient for spiritual maturity.

Notice also James's wording in verse 4: "Let patience have her perfect work." This is a command—something you must do. Furthermore, the grammar insists that it is to be going on continually in your life. Let endurance do its work in you constantly, especially while going through your trial. To put it another way, don't bail out of your trial!

Of course, that's not to say that it's wrong to seek relief. It's only natural to search out solutions to your problems. But all the while, you must be submissive to what God is doing in you through your trial. If you put all your trust and hope in solutions, you will likely be disheartened because the Lord wants to use your trial to draw you closer to him.

Some trials have exits. Since the Lord specializes in deliverances, those exits may be designed by him. However, the devil also hangs exit signs over doors, tempting you to bail out sooner than God wants. For example, divorce is one exit out of a troubled marriage. Suicide is an exit out of a health problem. Lying may prove to be an exit out of a sticky situation at work. But none of these is a God-approved exit. His counsel is: remain submissive under your trial. Every time you meet an exit door in a trial, you need to analyze it with the Word of God and prayer.

God's training

Hebrews 12:1-2 instructs us, "Wherefore seeing we also are compassed about with so great a cloud of witnesses, let us lay aside every weight, and the sin which doth so easily beset us, and let us run with patience the race that is set before us, looking unto Jesus the author and finisher of our faith; who for the joy that was set before him endured the cross, despising the shame, and is set down at the right hand of the throne of God." The word "patience" (v. 1) is the noun for the verb "endured" in verse 2. You are called to endure the race—to stay in it, remaining under whatever the hardship might be. That's part of submission!

The writer goes on to describe the training school in which God has enrolled his children; it is his school of discipline (vv. 3-6). He says that you must not despise "the chastening of the Lord" (v. 5). The word "chastening" refers to the training and education of children, which includes correction and instruction. If you "quit school" before it is complete, you will not develop the character that God is trying to work in you (v. 11). That's why you are called to submit to the Father (v. 9)—a submission which requires endurance.

Children do not grow to maturity overnight. It takes time. Likewise, God does not work his righteousness in your life through one sermon, one trial, or even one reading of the Bible. It is a life-long pursuit that requires daily submission. And since it lasts so long, you will need endurance.

When James Garfield, later to become President of the United States, was principal of Hiram College in Ohio, one father asked him if the course of his son's studies could not be shortened so that his son might be able to complete his studies in less time. "Certainly," replied Mr. Garfield. "But it all depends on what you want to make of your boy.

When God wants to make an oak, he takes one hundred years. When he wants to make a squash, he requires only two months."[22]

Too many times, you and I want instant success. After all, we live in an instant age: instant mashed potatoes, instant oatmeal, instant pudding, instant downloads, and instant transfers. But there's nothing instant about the Christian life, except the regeneration that begins it all. You won't become a mature Christian without submission anchored in perseverance. That's why perseverance is a critical color in the submission spectrum. It's what makes our submission long lasting.

Brother Andrew, known also as "God's Smuggler," carried thousands of Bibles behind the Iron Curtain when communist regimes were the strongest. In his autobiography, he tells about the persecuted believers that he met behind the curtain and the troubles that they faced on a daily basis. Romania was one of the worst countries with some of the most rigid control on churches. Naturally, this left many believers demoralized. In fact, many of them wanted nothing more than to get out of Romania.

But not all believers had this desire. Andrew met a family in Transylvania who owned a poultry farm. The state required that they meet a certain quota each year in order to keep their farm, but the requirement was beyond their ability. When they fell short, they had to buy eggs on the open market to make up the difference. This cut into their profit and hurt them economically.

Andrew asked them, "Why do you stay then? So that you can keep your farm?" "The farmer and his wife both looked shocked. 'Of course not,' he said. 'In fact, we certainly will lose the farm. We stay because—'he let his eyes travel across the valley—'because if we go, who will be left to pray?'"[23]

Having concluded that God wanted them to remain in a difficult land and having submitted to that will, they were ready to persevere even when it cost them their livelihood. That is perseverant submission.

CHAPTER 8 – CONTENTMENT

Ultimately, submission is more than *action*; it is an *attitude*. Therefore, the arrangement of your will under another is more than compliance—doing what you are told. True submission will reach the state of contentment. There are actually no verses in the Bible that bring together the words "content" and "submit," but the marriage of these two virtues is clearly illustrated in the lives of those who have developed true biblical submission. Therefore, I do not believe that the spiritual link can be denied.

Examples from Jesus' Life

Since Jesus is the best biblical example of perfect submission, you should not be surprised to find this color of submission expressed in his life. However, there is more subtlety in its demonstration than with the other colors.

As a child

We are indebted to Luke for the one account from Jesus' youth. The holy family had made their annual trek to Jerusalem for the Passover, and Jesus, caught up with the excitement of being in the Temple, lagged behind when his parents started for home. After missing Jesus for three days, they finally found him in the Temple. Out of panic, his mother scolded him, "Why have you treated us like this? We have been looking all over for you." Jesus' simple reply was, "Why were you looking for me? Didn't you know that I must be about my Father's business?" They did not understand this statement, and they must have said (as any parent would have), "Come on, it's time to go home."[24] Luke then records, "And he went down with them, and came to Nazareth, and was subject unto them" (Luke 2:51).

The word "subject" means "to submit." Thus, Luke assures us that there was no fight, no argument on Jesus' part. He submitted to them not only by going home to Nazareth but also by obeying all the other demands they made upon him. He fulfilled the fifth commandment perfectly: "Honor thy father and thy mother" (Exod. 20:12). At the age of twelve, Jesus had an urgency to do his Heavenly Father's work, but it was not yet time for him to begin that work. Contentedly, he submitted to his parents and returned home, taking up his place in the carpentry shop.[25]

How can we be certain that Jesus submitted contently? After all, I am sure that you have seen teenagers "submit" to their parents by complying with a miserable attitude—one meant to punish their parents for making them do something that they didn't want to do. I offer Luke 3:23 as proof. Here, Luke tells us that Jesus was about thirty when he began his ministry. In other words, Jesus remained in Nazareth, working in the carpentry shop alongside Joseph, for another eighteen years. That hardly describes a young man who was chomping at the bit to do what he wanted. Of course, Jesus' submission to his parents grew out of his greater submission to God.

In his ministry

While the disciples were in Sychar buying bread, Jesus remained at the well outside the city. There he spoke with a Samaritan woman, introducing her to the living water that would quench her thirsting soul, and she left as a believer in Jesus Christ. After she was gone, the disciples said to the Master, "Come and eat something." Jesus, never wishing to miss a teaching opportunity replied, "I have food to eat of which you do not know" (John 4:32 NKJV).

This statement confused the disciples. They were thinking literally; Jesus was speaking figuratively. Therefore, Jesus spoke plainly, "My food is to do the will of him who sent me" (v. 34 NKJV). One of the truths that Jesus wanted them to understand was that just as there is satisfaction in food, so he found satisfaction in doing the will of God. Jesus was content to do God's will whatever that may be.

Christ wants his followers to develop the same kind of thinking because he said in the very next verse, "Say not ye, There are yet four months, and then cometh harvest? behold, I say unto you, Lift up your eyes, and look on the fields; for they are white already to harvest" (v. 35). There is a natural link between the harvest and food, which suggests that reaping the harvest should result in satisfaction. Furthermore, Jesus' promise of reward (v. 36) should add to the satisfaction and contentment of doing God's will.

Is this the attitude that you have? Do you find satisfaction in fulfilling God's will? Are you content in your submission to that will?

Going to the cross

The greatest work of Jesus Christ was his atonement on the cross, but in this most difficult act of submission, he was content. In John 12:27, he prayed, "Now is my soul troubled; and what shall I say? 'Father, save me from this hour': but for this cause came I unto this hour." Jesus refused to ask the Father to save him from the "hour" for which he had come into the world—his death on the cross. But was he perfectly content, or was this merely passive compliance? After all, many men and women, both godly and ungodly, have accepted death with passive resignation.

The remainder of Jesus' prayer leaves no doubt. Christ continued, "'Father, glorify thy name.' Then came there a voice from heaven, saying, 'I have both glorified it, and will glorify it again'" (v. 28). Jesus' focus was on glorifying God. In the next chapter, John records that as soon as Judas left the Upper Room, Jesus, knowing that Judas intended to betray him, stated, "Now is the Son of man glorified, and God is glorified in him" (John 13:31). The gears were now turning; the events that would bring Christ to the cross were in motion. But at this pivotal moment, the focus of the Savior was not on his suffering or even on his obedience. Christ's focus was on the glory of God. Jesus knew that his death would bring glory to God, which in turn would bring glory to him.

Therefore, as Jesus faced the cross on that fateful night, he was not unsubmissive or even reticently submissive. Jesus exulted in the glory of God. Leon Morris keenly observes, "The glory of the Father is bound up with the glory of the Son. The two are one in the purpose of saving sinners. The glory of Christ as he stoops to save us is the glory of the Father whose will he is doing. The cross reveals the heart of God as well as that of Christ."[26] Since his heart embraced the cross, Jesus was content to die there in God's will.

The Heart in Submission

True submission must come to the place of contentment. It's more than resignation or compliance. The *heart* must embrace the submission, not just the *will*.

I was counseling Jacob[27] concerning his summer plans when he decided that God wanted him to travel with an evangelist. But that choice needed the approval of his parents before it could become a reality. The final decision was not his own, and Jacob was obligated to submit to whatever they said. I knew this was right since parents are in the place of authority and often see the bigger picture better than teenagers. But I also knew that many teens would resent such submission, especially if their parents came to a different conclusion.

When I realized what Jacob was facing, my greatest concern was for his heart, so I asked him, "Are you OK with that?" Jacob paused in his usual thoughtful way, and then, looking straight at me, he said, "Yes." I knew by the tone of his voice and the agreement in his eyes that he was submissively content. It was one of those moments when I sat back and marveled at him for I knew that I could not have answered as contentedly as he had if I had been in his shoes.

It was not the first time I had seen such vivid contentment in submission. I encountered it years before in my mother-in-law. When my wife's parents first moved to Texas, they lived in a bus—a commercial coach bus designed like an RV on the inside. They were still living in the bus four years later when my wife and I visited them after we were married. Such cramped quarters would have been enough to drive any woman crazy, but my dear mother-in-law found contentment. She said, "I figure that if I learn to stay organized in this bus, the Lord might give me something bigger someday." No complaining. No nagging. No pining for something better.

That's true submission. To accept your lot without complaining. To say about the decision that God makes for you or the circumstance he allows in your life, "I'm OK with that." But how do you get to that place?

Finding Contentment

Three times, the Apostle Paul asked the Lord to take away his thorn in the flesh, but the Lord refused. Three times, he answered, "My grace is sufficient for thee: for my strength is made perfect in weakness." Paul was required to submit to his thorn. Did he do so with bitterness or contentment? The Apostle wrote, "Most gladly therefore will I rather glory in my infirmities, that the power of Christ may rest upon me" (2 Cor. 12:9). Obviously, there is contentment in those words "most gladly"!

The key to Paul's contentment in a difficult, unwanted circumstance was Christ's promise to him: "My grace is sufficient." The word "sufficient" means "to be adequate with the implication of leading to satisfaction."[28] The word is also translated "content" in the New Testament:

- "Be **content** with your wages." (Luke 3:14)
- "Two hundred pennyworth of bread is not **sufficient.**" (John 6:7)
- "Be **content** with such things as ye have." (Heb. 13:5)

Let's describe these three occurrences in terms of adequacy. John the Baptist told the soldiers, "Your wages are enough." The disciples protested at feeding the five thousand people by saying, "Two hundred denarii worth of bread is not enough." And the writer of Hebrews pointedly declared, "What you have is enough."

Christ's promise to Paul and to you is "My grace is enough! You don't need relief. You don't need anything else." And when you come to accept that Christ's grace is truly enough, you will be able to say with Paul, even about debilitating thorns, "I'm OK with that."

Do you realize that you do this for salvation because you *know* that there is nothing you can do to save yourself? You fall upon God's grace and say, "It is enough. I don't need anything else—no works, no religious rites." God's grace is sufficient to save you. And Christ wants you to accept his sufficient grace in other matters, as well.

- *It's OK that I can't fix my crisis. God's grace will see me through.*
- *It's OK that I can't cure my loved one. God's grace will see me through.*
- *It's OK that the government is creating more headaches for me. God's grace will see me through.*
- *It's OK that my child will not be all that I dreamed he would be. God's grace will see me through.*

This is not a fatalistic resignation to the problem. In fatalism, one embraces the thorn. You are called to embrace Christ's grace, and that brings supernatural strength, causing God to get the glory. Christ said to Paul, "My strength is made perfect in weakness." And when you are living for the glory of God even in your weaknesses, you are demonstrating Christ-likeness because that is what he was doing as he prayed in the Upper Room hours before bearing his own cross.

The Message of the New Year
I asked the New Year for some motto sweet,
Some rule of life with which to guide my feet;
I asked, and paused; he answered soft and low:
"God's will to know."

"Will knowledge then suffice, New Year?" I cried;
And, ere the question into silence died,
The answer came: "Nay, but remember, too,
God's will to do."

Once more I asked, "Is there no more to tell?"
And once again the answer sweetly fell:
"Yes! this one thing, all other things above,
God's will to love."
—*Anonymous*[29]

It is one thing to *know* God's will. It is a better thing to *do* God's will. But the greatest of all is to *love* God's will. Such is the attitude of contentment.

CHAPTER 9 – JOY

J oy. It seems to be the one virtue that everyone pursues. Even our forefathers believed that the pursuit of happiness was an unalienable right,[30] and ever since those words were penned in Philadelphia in 1776, Americans have lived them ardently. But man's pursuit of joy is usually self-centered. "What makes me happy?" is the question he asks himself. In fact, this is one of the most common messages of Hollywood. You will hear statements like, "Just follow your heart." But is that the true path to joy? The warnings of the Bible abound concerning that kind of pursuit. It declares rather that joy is found on a different path—an unexpected path. Joy is found on the pathway of submission.

Joy is a Fruit.

The first thing that you must understand is that joy is a fruit. And fruit is a result—something that comes after certain conditions are fulfilled. If you expect fruit from your apple trees, blueberry bushes, or tomato plants, you know that certain conditions must be met. There must be water, sunshine, warmth, cultivation, and time. Likewise, joy is a fruit; it doesn't "just happen" in your life.

Paul says that joy is part of the fruit of the Spirit (Gal. 5:22); thus, it is something that the Spirit of God works in you. That explains why true joy will not be achieved in the self-centered life. God's Spirit wants nothing to do with that type of living.

What are the conditions for producing joy?

In the analogy of the vine, Jesus answers that question succinctly. He says, "If ye keep my commandments, ye shall abide in my love; even as I have kept my Father's commandments, and abide in his love. These things have I spoken unto you, that my joy might remain in you, and that your joy might be full" (John 15:10-11).

The words "these things have I spoken" refer back to the call to obedience in the previous verse. In other words, obeying Christ's commands results in joy—a joy filled to the brim. Since these verses are spoken in the context of the vine and branches, Jesus is describing fruit and the conditions for it.

Have you ever visited a desert? It's miles of wasteland, where little grows. That's the idea that many people have about submission to God. They imagine that to submit to God means they will live in a personal wasteland where refreshment and beauty are scarce. If you listen to some Christians who *say* they are in submission to the will of God, you get the impression that such a place is full of sorrow and misery. But this is not what Jesus promises. He describes the life of submissive obedience as a fruitful vine and a cup full of joy. It's like living in the Garden of Eden, which was "well watered every where" (Gen. 13:10). Leon Morris says, "It is no cheerless, barren existence that Jesus plans for his people."[31]

I don't mean to give you the idea that there is never hardship or sorrow in submission to God. The Bible never depicts that false portrayal. Consider the lives of the prophets, the ministries of the apostles, and above all, the experience of Jesus himself. All of these submissive men knew their share of trouble.

The promise of Scripture is that sorrow and pain give way to joy in the Christian experience—a joy that is permanent. As he faced his own dark hour and tried to prepare his disciples for theirs, Jesus reminded them, "A woman when she is in travail hath sorrow, because her hour is come: but as soon as she is delivered of the child, she remembereth no more the anguish, for joy that a man is born into the world. And ye now therefore have sorrow: but I will see you again, and your heart shall rejoice, and your joy no man taketh from you" (John 16:21-22).

This was the experience of the disciples as they lived through the crucifixion of Christ followed by his resurrection. This also proved to be their experience throughout life. Paul testified, "I am filled with comfort; I am exceeding joyful in all our tribulation" (2 Cor. 7:4).

John teaches that joy is the fruit of fellowship with God (1 John 1:3-6). Fellowship with God is lost only by sin (disobedience to God's commands). Therefore, when you sin, you lose your joy. Such was the experience of David (Ps. 51:12). That is why you are urged to confess your sins and be restored to fellowship with God (1 John 1:9). But since your fellowship with God is hindered only by an inner problem (sin) and not by outward circumstances, your joy need not be lost just because life gets hard. Thus, submission to God—even in very difficult circumstances—does not mean a life without joy. Therefore, when you hear Christians with a tone of grumbled unhappiness claim to be submitted to God, you can be certain that theirs is not a Christ-like submission.

This brings us to a second startling truth about joy.

Joy is a Choice.

Now, you may be saying, "A choice? I thought joy was a feeling, and I can't very easily choose my feelings." But that's where the misconception lies. There are certainly feelings with joy, but joy is not solely a feeling.

James writes, "My brethren, count it all joy when ye fall into divers temptations" (1:2). The word "count" is a cognitive word. It means to consider or think about something based not so much upon feelings but upon facts. James says that when you face trials of various kinds, you should be able to consider it all joy because of the facts about trials. He goes on to describe some of those facts: endurance and spiritual maturity (vv. 3-4). James is not ignoring the pain; he's telling you to look beyond it to the joy.

When you truly bring your heart to submissive surrender through trust, humility, and reverence and follow it up with perseverance and contentment, you won't have any problem seeing the joy. That's how joy is a choice.

John the Baptist's testimony is an excellent example. As the popularity of Jesus Christ grew, John's followers left him. His crowds dwindled. His candidates for baptism diminished. His disciples worried that his ministry was going to collapse, but John was not bothered. John knew that he must submit to Christ, and that meant he was going to decrease while Christ increased (John 3:29-30). Most men would have become jealous or at least discouraged. But John said, "My joy is fulfilled" (v. 29). In other words, he had been living and working for that moment.

To illustrate his point, John described Jesus as the groom and himself as the best man. At a wedding, few people take notice of the best man (unless he forgets the ring). The bride and groom are rightfully the center of attention. But that does not diminish the joy of the best man in any measure. I have been a best man only once in my life, and that was for my brother. As I stood with him on that stage, it was a happy day for me. I rejoiced that God had given him a loving wife. I was not sad, and I did not wish for people to notice me. It was his day, and he deserved all the happiness that that day could bestow.

The point is that joy is a choice that you make by the focus you decide to maintain. John had joy because his focus was on Christ's increase, not on his decrease. If in your submission, your focus is on God and the eternal, you also will experience joy.

Jesus' Joy in Submission

As he urges you to run the race, the writer of Hebrews holds up the example of Jesus. He says, "Looking unto Jesus the author and finisher of our faith; who for the joy that was set before him endured the cross, despising the shame, and is set down at the right hand of the throne of God" (Heb. 12:2). In his greatest act of submission, Jesus endured the cross because of the "joy that was set before him."

Christ's joy was first a choice. The book of Hebrews attributes the words of Psalm 40:8 as a prophecy of Christ. He is made to say, "I delight to do thy will, O my God: yea, thy law is within my heart." To submit to the will of God was Jesus' greatest pleasure, and that was true even when he faced the cross. The word translated "delight" in Psalm 40:8 is the same Hebrew word translated "pleased" in Isaiah 53:10: "Yet it pleased the LORD to bruise him." Let that sink in. The Father was *pleased* to bruise his Son in order to save man, and the Son was *pleased* to accept the bruising for man's redemption.

Jesus Christ had arranged Himself so perfectly under the Father that he had no will apart from God's. He said, "I seek not mine own will, but the will of the Father which hath sent me" (John 5:30). If you have ever tried to tune two instruments, you know you have succeeded when the notes from both instruments blend into one voice. If they are not in tune, you can hear acoustical beats between the two notes, but these beats disappear when they are matched perfectly. Jesus experienced that kind of perfect submission. His will blended so perfectly with His Father's that there was no dissonance between them.

The fruit of his obedient submission was joy. Hebrews says that the joy was set before him. Christ could look beyond the suffering and pain to the joy that awaited him. Jesus taught his disciples, "Verily, verily, I say unto you, Except a corn of wheat fall into the ground and die, it abideth alone: but if it die, it bringeth forth much fruit" (John 12:24). After his resurrection, he declared, "Ought not Christ to have suffered these things, and to enter into his glory?" (Luke 24:26). The writer of Hebrews called Christ the captain of our salvation who through his submission was "bringing many sons unto glory" (2:10). The fruit, the glory, and the eternal souls who would be saved were all part of the "joy that was set before him." He chose the path of submission because he knew it was also the path of joy. And so, all the colors of submission are perfectly displayed in Jesus Christ—from his arrangement under the Father to his eternal joy.

What is true of Christ can be true of you. Jesus appeals to you, "These things have I spoken unto you, that my joy might remain in you, and that your joy might be full" (John 15:11). The joy that Christ promises you is not imprecise and impersonal. It is *his* joy—the joy that he experienced in submission, the joy that took him to the cross for your sins, the joy that he knew in resurrection triumph. This is the joy that he offers you when you choose the same path of obedient submission.

In her book *Green Leaf in Drought,* Isobel Kuhn tells the story of Arthur and Wilda Mathews, the last China Inland Mission missionaries to escape from Communist China. The Mathews had willingly surrendered to take the Gospel to the Chinese, but when the Communists took over in the early 1950s, it soon became apparent that they were not going to be given the freedom to preach. Therefore, they applied to the government for exit visas. It took two years before their visas were granted. During that time of waiting, the Communists attempted to threaten them, compromise them, falsely accuse them, and even starve them by freezing all their funds. As time wore on, even the Chinese Christians withdrew from them, leaving them quite isolated and impoverished. It was a severe trial for both of them, and they often became discouraged. They just couldn't understand why God was not allowing them to leave China since they couldn't do anything there for God. They felt as if they had been given a bitter cup to drink.

Tenderly, the Lord brought both of them at separate times to recognize that he wanted more than dutiful obedience. He wanted them to delight in his will. When the day came that Arthur and Wilda knelt and finally abandoned themselves to God's will even if that meant staying in China indefinitely, their hearts were flooded with joy. Later Arthur wrote, "We are no longer stupid bullocks being driven or dragged unwillingly along a distasteful road; but sons, co-operating wholeheartedly with our Father." Recalling the picture from which she derived the title of her book, Kuhn comments,

> *Here we see the bursting of the green.* Up to now, with all the drought and parched ground, the little trees have sent out a green leaf or two, to show that life was not quenched. But as happens when the sap has full unhindered course to run throughout trunk and branches, there comes a day when all over the tree, green buds are sprouting, bursting forth.[32]

Perfect submission is not experienced in the surrender. That is only the beginning of submission and very imperfect like the first leaf that appears on a tree. Perfect submission is experienced when the soul finds joy in that submission. It is then that you see the "bursting of the green" and all the colors of submission.

CONCLUSION – PERFECT SUBMISSION

Perfect Submission—all is at rest,
I in my Savior am happy and blest.[33]

These words of Fanny Crosby remind us that without perfect submission all will not be at rest. Without submission, you are at odds with the Lord in some area of your life, and that will disturb your peace. Her words also hint at another truth that I hope you have gleaned from the previous pages of this book. Only Jesus Christ has lived his entire life in perfect submission. Therefore, you will need to strive for that Christ-likeness if you are going to reach perfect submission. But the good news is that with Christ living within you, it can be done.

Yet, I hasten to add that this is a growing process. As I mentioned in the preface of this book, I am still trying to learn it. Actually, I find myself more submissive on some days than others—just as some days I find it easier to desire and pursue holiness than others. As long as we are on this side of Glory, our flesh is a constant hindrance. But do not let that stop you from pressing toward the mark (Phil. 3:14).

The purpose of this book has been to make the pursuit of that perfect submission a little easier by breaking the virtue down into its various facets or colors. Whenever I find myself struggling to submit to God in some area, I review the colors to locate which has grown pale in my life. To illustrate what this may look like, permit me to share a very personal example.

My wife and I were unable to have any children of our own, so we decided to adopt a child from Russia. Nathanael was seven months old when we brought him home, and we were very excited parents. Although he was delayed developmentally due to his early months in an orphanage, the first few years progressed as expected. But when he turned four, problems began to surface. These problems increased in intensity over the next several years, prodding us to find answers and help for our son. Finally, we received a medical diagnosis. Nathanael has fetal alcohol spectrum disorder, which means that he has irreversible brain damage because of prenatal exposure to alcohol.

The prognoses of children on the spectrum vary. Some may be able to function very well independently; others will not. Nathanael's future is still unknown to us, and we continue to do the best that we can as parents to rear him for God's glory. But I will admit that there are times when I find myself struggling with God's choice for us. As my friends share about the remarkable accomplishments of their teenage children, I am reminded of how much my son has yet to learn—or may never learn. While other fathers are teaching their sons how to mow the lawn, drive a car, or to be a leader, I am still working with my teenager on simple daily functions, such as how to brush his teeth, wash his face, and have appropriate conversations.

Before the Lord gave us our son, I had hopes and dreams for my child as any father would. I hoped he could go to college at my alma mater. I dreamed about what career or ministry he might be able to do. I even anticipated grandchildren...way off in the future. Sometimes those dreams come back to haunt me, and those are the moments when I find myself struggling with my submission to God's will. I've asked the questions "Why" and "Why not" more than I should.

In those moments when things are not all at rest in my soul, I remind myself of the colors of submission. I need surrender. Yes, that's a common one in my life. But why do I struggle in surrendering to God? Maybe I'm not trusting him as I should. As I analyze my heart, I may find worry, which needs to be confessed and my trust renewed. More often, I find pride, and I need to humble myself before my sovereign God, who wrote the story of my life long before I ever tried. As I look at dashed and broken dreams, I usually find that the color of contentment has gone pale. I then need to remind myself that it's OK for my dreams to die; God's grace will be enough.

By focusing on those specific colors of need and purposely trying to emulate my Savior in those areas of my life, I find it easier to submit. I'll admit that it is usually painful because I'm putting self to death. But as I find myself closer to perfect submission, I see Christ's likeness being formed in me, and that brings great rejoicing to my soul.

May God do the same for you!

APPENDIX

Verses on Submission

Below is a complete list of all the verses in the New Testament where the verb *hupotassō* appears. I offer them to you without comment, but I have bolded the English word that translates the Greek verb to enable you to see it more quickly.

Luke 2:51
And he went down with them, and came to Nazareth, and **was subject** unto them: but his mother kept all these sayings in her heart.

Luke 10:17
And the seventy returned again with joy, saying, Lord, even the devils **are subject** unto us through thy name.

Luke 10:20
Notwithstanding in this rejoice not, that the spirits **are subject** unto you; but rather rejoice, because your names are written in heaven.

Romans 8:7
Because the carnal mind is enmity against God: for it **is** not **subject** to the law of God, neither indeed can be.

Romans 8:20
For the creature **was made subject** to vanity, not willingly, but by reason of him who **hath subjected** the same in hope,

Romans 10:3
For they being ignorant of God's righteousness, and going about to establish their own righteousness, **have** not **submitted** themselves unto the righteousness of God.

Romans 13:1
Let every soul **be subject** unto the higher powers. For there is no power but of God: the powers that be are ordained of God.

Romans 13:5
Wherefore ye must needs **be subject**, not only for wrath, but also for conscience sake.

1 Corinthians 14:32
And the spirits of the prophets **are subject** to the prophets.

1 Corinthians 14:34
Let your women keep silence in the churches: for it is not permitted unto them to speak; but they are commanded to **be under obedience**, as also saith the law.

1 Corinthians 15:27
For he **hath put** all things **under** his feet. But when he saith all things are **put under** him, it is manifest that he is excepted, which did **put** all things **under** him.

1 Corinthians 15:28
And when all things shall **be subdued** unto him, then shall the Son also himself **be subject** unto him that **put** all things **under** him, that God may be all in all.

1 Corinthians 16:16
That ye **submit** yourselves unto such, and to every one that helpeth with us, and laboreth.

Ephesians 1:22
And **hath put** all things **under** his feet, and gave him to be the head over all things to the church,

Ephesians 5:21
Submitting yourselves one to another in the fear of God.

Ephesians 5:22
Wives, **submit** yourselves unto your own husbands, as unto the Lord.

Ephesians 5:24
Therefore as the church **is subject** unto Christ, so let the wives be to their own husbands in every thing.

Philippians 3:21
Who shall change our vile body, that it may be fashioned like unto his glorious body, according to the working whereby he is able even to **subdue** all things unto himself.

Colossians 3:18
Wives, **submit** yourselves unto your own husbands, as it is fit in the Lord.

Titus 2:5
To be discreet, chaste, keepers at home, good, **obedient** to their own husbands, that the word of God be not blasphemed.

Titus 2:9
Exhort servants to **be obedient** unto their own masters, and to please them well in all things; not answering again;

Titus 3:1
Put them in mind to **be subject** to principalities and powers, to obey magistrates, to be ready to every good work,

Hebrews 2:5
For unto the angels hath he not **put in subjection** the world to come, whereof we speak.

Hebrews 2:8
Thou hast **put** all things **in subjection** under his feet. For in that he **put** all **in subjection under** him, he left nothing that is not put under him. But now we see not yet all things **put under** him.

Hebrews 12:9
Furthermore we have had fathers of our flesh which corrected us, and we gave them reverence: shall we not much rather **be in subjection** unto the Father of spirits, and live?

James 4:7
Submit yourselves therefore to God. Resist the devil, and he will flee from you.

1 Peter 2:13
Submit yourselves to every ordinance of man for the Lord's sake: whether it be to the king, as supreme;

1 Peter 2:18
Servants, **be subject** to your masters with all fear; not only to the good and gentle, but also to the froward.

1 Peter 3:1
Likewise, ye wives, **be in subjection** to your own husbands; that, if any obey not the word, they also may without the word be won by the conversation of the wives;

1 Peter 3:5
For after this manner in the old time the holy women also, who trusted in God, adorned themselves, **being in subjection** unto their own husbands:

1 Peter 3:22
Who is gone into heaven, and is on the right hand of God; angels and authorities and powers being **made subject** unto him.

1 Peter 5:5
Likewise, ye younger, **submit** yourselves unto the elder. Yea, all of you **be subject** one to another, and be clothed with humility: for God resisteth the proud, and giveth grace to the humble.

The noun *hupotagé* appears in four verses:

2 Corinthians 9:13
Whiles by the experiment of this ministration they glorify God for your professed **subjection** unto the gospel of Christ, and for your liberal distribution unto them, and unto all men;

Galatians 2:5
To whom we gave place by **subjection**, no, not for an hour; that the truth of the gospel might continue with you.

1 Timothy 2:11
Let the woman learn in silence with all **subjection**.

1 Timothy 3:4
One that ruleth well his own house, having his children in **subjection** with all gravity;

STUDY GUIDE

Chapter 1 - Arrangement

1. Describe why arrangement is a necessary component of submission?

2. List at least three things that are subject to Jesus.

3. Give two examples from Jesus' life that show his submissive arrangement to the Father.

4. Look back at the seven life relationships requiring submission and read the corresponding verses (p. 8). Do you struggle with any of these relationships? If so, describe which one(s) and what makes submission hard for you.

5. Re-read this statement from page 9: "Your submission in other relationships of life ultimately is a reflection of your submission to God." With that in mind, consider your answer in the previous question, and describe what your submission to God looks like.

6. Arrangement in submission involves being perfectly aligned under God. Is there something that God has put in your life that you are struggling to accept as His perfect will for you? If so, why?

7. Memorize James 4:7.

Memorization Hints:

- If you struggle to memorize verses, try writing them out on 3x5 cards and reading them out loud 3 times a day for a week or until you can say them.

- It might also be helpful to write the first letter of each word in the verse on a cue card to guide your review. James 4:7 (KJV) would look like this: S y t t G. R t d, a h w f f y.

Chapter 2 - Obedience

1. Why must obedience follow arrangement?

2. Who is unable to submit to God's law? Why?

3. How does one receive a change of heart that is necessary for obedience to God? Is this something you have received?

4. Is there an area in your life where you are struggling or refusing to obey God? Is there a sin you need to forsake? What act of obedience would replace it?

5. What is the test of submission?

6. How did Jesus show obedient submission? How can you follow in his steps?

7. According to God's Word, when are you to obey your earthly authorities?

8. Proverbs 3:17 says of God's wisdom: "Her ways are ways of pleasantness, and all her paths are peace." Is this the way you feel about the path of obedience?

9. Memorize Romans 6:13.

Chapter 3 - Surrender

1. List two reasons why we struggle to surrender?

2. What will happen if you do not surrender to God?

3. Name the two things that Jesus relied upon to reach the place of full surrender?

4. Consider your answers from Question 6 in Chapter 1 and Question 4 in Chapter 2. Identify the area in your life in which you have not surrendered?

5. Find at least two Bible verses that apply to your lack of surrender and meditate on them.

6. Write a prayer telling God what you learned from his Word and asking him to help you accept his deliberate decisions for your life.

7. Memorize Luke 22:42.

Chapter 4 - Trust

1. Explain the link between submission and trust.

2. In surrendering to God's will, how did Jesus specifically display his trust in God?

3. What does Abraham teach us about the secret of willing surrender?

4. Re-read this statement from page 25: "Until you settle the matter in your heart that you can trust God no matter what happens, you will always struggle to surrender to him." Consider again your area of struggle that you identified in Question 4 of Chapter 3. Does this struggle proceed from a lack of trust in God? If so, which attribute of God do you need to learn to trust (e.g., his goodness, love, wisdom, omnipotence, etc.)?

5. Write down at least three verses that teach about the attribute you chose. Ask God to help you know him better and to learn to surrender to him in trust.

6. Memorize Proverbs 29:25.

Suggested Resources on the Attributes of God:

> *The Knowledge of the Holy* by A. W. Tozer
> *Lord, I Want to Know You* by Kay Arthur
> *Names of God* by Nathan Stone
> *Trusting God* by Jerry Bridges

Chapter 5 - Humility

1. What is the biblical connection between humility and submission?

2. Re-read Philippians 2:5-8 and the verses from John on page 33, and describe Christ's submissive humility to the plan of God.

3. Andrew Murray wrote of Christ's humility that it was "the surrender of himself to God, to allow the Father to do in him what he pleased." Think again of that area in which you are struggling to surrender to God. Describe the pride in your resistance. Are you willing to resign your desires humbly and accept God's sovereign will to do as he pleases?

4. Is there any person with whom you do not get along? Ask the Lord to show you three selfless things that you could do in this relationship. Write down those actions.

5. Choose one verse from this chapter to memorize and explain why you chose it.

Chapter 6 - Reverence

1. Name the three relationships where the Bible links reverence with submission.

2. Do your priorities show that you acknowledge God's rightful place in your life? List in order your top three priorities and how they influence your time, money, and/or actions. Do your priorities align with the priorities set forth in God's Word?

3. Are you struggling to reverence God by not accepting a decision of God in your life (e.g., health issue, family crisis, tragic loss, etc.)?

4. A lack of reverence in submitting to God or other relationships shows a lack of love. List specific ways in which your love for God shows in your life. What more can you do to demonstrate your love for God?

5. Read John 17. Give three verses from Jesus' prayer that show a submission springing out of reverence to God.

6. Memorize Deuteronomy 6:5.

Chapter 7 - Perseverance

1. Underline the three most significant statements to you in this chapter.

2. Based on what you have learned from this chapter, how would you describe perseverance in submission?

3. Name three of the most difficult areas in your life in which perseverance in submission is necessary. Give a specific example of one of these.

4. Re-read the list of sufferings that Jesus endured to purchase your redemption (p. 46). How does his perseverance provide you an example to persevere in the areas you listed in Question 3.

5. In the trials of life, unconditional surrender begins with a decision, but it has to be carried out continually in daily life. You may be growing weary and feeling as if you can't go on anymore. Meditate on 1 Corinthians 15:58, Galatians 6:9, Philippians 3:14, Hebrews 12:1-2, and James 1:1-4. Write down a truth from one of these verses to keep you focused on perseverance.

6. Memorize James 1:2-4.

Chapter 8 - Contentment

1. How did Jesus show contentment in submission?

2. What promise of Christ needs to be embraced to find contentment in submission?

3. What is the difference between fatalistic resignation and contentment?

4. The chapter concludes with this statement: "It is one thing to *know* God's will. It is a better thing to *do* God's will. But the greatest of all is to *love* God's will." Can you honestly say that you *love* God's will? If not, what steps should you take to grow in contentment?

5. Are you content with God's will for your life, including the areas you named in Question 3 of Chapter 7? What do you want that you don't have?

6. Describe what contentment in submission should look like in the areas you named in the previous question.

7. Memorize 2 Corinthians 12:9.

Chapter 9 - Joy

1. Explain why submission to God, even in the midst of trials, should not mean a life without joy.

2. Is there a prevailing circumstance in your life that seems to rob you consistently of your joy? Or to put it another way, how would you fill in the following blank? "If only _____, I could be joyful."

3. In James 1:2, what does the word "count" mean?

4. How is joy a choice, especially in submission?

5. Describe the joy in Jesus' submission.

6. Consider your answer in Question 2. How can you count this circumstance all joy? How can you choose Christ's joy in this instance?

7. Memorize Hebrews 12:2.

Conclusion - Perfect Submission

1. List the nine colors of submission (p. 3) and memorize them.

2. Review the areas that you have identified in which it is difficult for you to submit. Which color of submission has grown pale in your life? What can you start doing to make it vibrant again?

3. Describe the growth you are seeing in your life towards perfect submission?

4. Write a truth you have learned, and describe how the Lord has given you the strength to apply it in your life.

5. Memorize 1 Peter 2:21. Ask the Lord, by his grace, to make it your ongoing desire to grow in submission so that you may follow in his steps.

NOTES

1 *An Expository Dictionary of New Testament Words*, s.v. "Subject," by W. E. Vine (Westwood, NJ: Fleming H. Revell Co., 1966).

2 Ray Overholt, *Ten Thousand Angels* (Brentwood, TN: Lillenas Publishing Co., 1959).

3 The references listed here are only a sampling. Many other verses could be added to these. See Appendix. It is well worth the study to categorize them by relationship.

4 Dwight Lyman Moody, *1,100 Illustrations form the Writings of D. L. Moody*, ed. John W. Reed (Grand Rapids, MI: Baker Books, 1996), 285-86.

5 Mrs. A. A. Whiddington, *Not I, But Christ*.

6 Paul Lee Tan, ed., *Encyclopedia of 15,000 Illustrations* (Signs of the Times, 1998), Word*search* digital edition, entry #12652.

7 This is actually one word in the original, an intensification of the word "sorrowful" in verse 37.

8 John Foxe, *Foxe's Book of Martyrs* (Complete and unabridged, Word*search* digital edition), Chapter 16, "Archbishop Cranmer."

9 My paraphrase of Jeremiah 38:17-18.

10 *Theléma*

11 *Boulomai*

12 Cf. Exodus 18:7, 1 Kings 19:18, and 2 Samuel 15:5, where the practice is actually backwards. Absalom won the hearts of the people because he bowed and kissed *them* rather than requiring them to do it to him as would have been the custom.

13 The name *Jehovah-Jireh* means "The Lord will provide."

14 Andrew Murray, *Humility* (New Kensington, PA: Whitaker House, 1982), 22.

15 Murray, 22-23.

16 Murray, 23-24.

17 John MacArthur, Jr., *Found: God's Will* (Wheaton, IL: Victor Books, 1981), 39-40.

18 Murray, 23.

[19] Joni Eareckson Tada and Steven Estes, *When God Weeps: Why Our Sufferings Matter to the Almighty* (Grand Rapids, MI: Zondervan, 1997), 21.

[20] Leon Morris, *The Gospel According to John*, Rev. ed., The New International Commentary on the New Testament (Grand Rapids, MI: William B. Eerdmans Publishing Co., 1995), 635.

[21] The Greek word is *hupomoné*. The KJV translators preferred to translate the word "patience," but as this typically communicates a forbearance in waiting to speakers today, the more fitting word for modern English is "endurance."

[22] Paul Lee Tan, entry #2958.

[23] Brother Andrew and John and Elizabeth Sherrill, *God's Smuggler* (Old Tappan, NJ: Flemming H. Revell Co., 1967), 153 and 159.

[24] My paraphrase of Luke 2:41-50.

[25] See Mark 6:3.

[26] Morris, 560.

[27] For an introduction to Jacob and his role in the writing of this book, please see the preface.

[28] The Greek verb is *arkeō*. Cleon L. Rogers, Jr. and Cleon L. Rogers III, *The New Linguistic Key to the Greek New Testament* (Grand Rapids, MI: Zondervan Publishing House, 1998), 417.

[29] "The Message of the New Year," in *Rhyme and Reason*, ed. Bob Jones (Greenville, SC: Bob Jones University Press, 1981), 126.

[30] Preamble of the *United States Declaration of Independence*.

[31] Morris, 598.

[32] Isobel Kuhn, *Green Leaf in Drought* (Littleton, CO: OMF Books, 2001), 78-80.

[33] Fanny Crosby, *Blessed Assurance*.

85458905R00055

Made in the USA
Middletown, DE
24 August 2018